CHASING SHADOWS

A SPECIAL AGENT'S LIFELONG HUNT TO
BRING A COLD WAR ASSASSIN TO JUSTICE

FRED BURTON
AND JOHN BRUNING

palgrave

First published in hardcover in 2011 by PALGRAVE MACMILLAN®
in the US—a division of St. Martin's Press LLC, 175 Fifth Avenue,
New York, NY 10010.

Where this book is distributed in the UK, Europe and the rest of the
world, this is by Palgrave Macmillan, a division of Macmillan
Publishers Limited, registered in England, company number 785998, of
Houndmills, Basingstoke, Hampshire RG21 6XS.

Palgrave Macmillan is the global academic imprint of the above
companies and has companies and representatives throughout the
world.

Palgrave® and Macmillan® are registered trademarks in the United
States, the United Kingdom, Europe and other countries.

ISBN: 978-0-230-33991-0

The Library of Congress has catalogued the hardcover edition as
follows:

Burton, Fred.
   Chasing shadows : a special agent's lifelong hunt to bring a Cold War
assassin to justice / Fred Burton and John Bruning.
      p.   cm.
   Includes bibliographical references.
   ISBN 978-0-230-62055-1 (hardback)
   1. Burton, Fred. 2. Intelligence officers—United States—Biography.
3. Murder—Investigation—Case studies. 4. Alon, Joseph, d. 1973—
Assassination. 5. Intelligence officers—Israel—Biography.
6. Murder—Maryland—Bethesda—History—20th century.
7. Munazzamat Aylul al-Aswad. 8. Terrorism—Prevention—Case
studies. 9. Conspiracies—Case studies. 10. Cold War. I. Bruning,
John R. II. Title.
JK468.I6B888   2011
364.152'3092—dc22

                                                           2010038120

A catalogue record of the book is available from the British Library.

Design by Letra Libre

First PALGRAVE MACMILLAN paperback edition: May 2012

10 9 8 7 6 5 4 3 2 1

Printed in the United States of America.

This book is dedicated to the late Mark Broxmeyer,
an American patriot and a very good friend of Israel

CONTENTS

Eight pages of black-and-white photos
appear between pages 140 and 141.

PROLOGUE
THE LONG PURSUIT

On the night between June 30 and July 1, 1973, a man named Joseph Alon was murdered in the quiet suburban neighborhood only a few blocks from my house in Bethesda, Maryland. I was sixteen at the time, and I still remember sitting down to breakfast the morning after and reading of it in our local paper.[1] The aftershocks of that violent summer night resonated through my community for weeks. Not until much later did I realize that the shock waves were not limited to Bethesda and my narrow little world.

That July morning became a turning point in my own life. It was the first time violence had intruded on the one place I felt most safe: home. I had a dim understanding that, outside Bethesda's city limits, the world was on fire. Here in the quiet, leafy suburbs, however, we were supposed to be immune to such things.

We were not, and it was a tough lesson to absorb at sixteen. The sense of vulnerability I felt at the time was one of the reasons I chose a career in law enforcement. Later I joined the Diplomatic Security Service (DSS) as a counterterrorism agent.[2] Through the

1980s and 1990s, my career took me to every hot spot and violence-plagued region in the world. I worked cases that made front-page news across the globe, including the pursuit of such noted terrorists as Ramzi Yousef, the original World Trade Center bomber.

But I never forgot the one case that shattered my illusion of safety. I had looked into it when I first joined the Montgomery County Police Department (which is in Maryland, near Washington, D.C.) in 1981 and found the case file full of curious dead ends.[3] The crime had never been solved. By the mid-1970s, the case had been virtually forgotten.

While with the DSS, I dug deeper into the case files and discovered that this was no random act of violence. Eventually I acquired the entire file from the Federal Bureau of Investigation (FBI) as well as diplomatic documents related to the case.[4] The more I learned, the more questions I had. Over the years, I worked on the case whenever I had a free moment—a night here, an afternoon there. The leads I developed shocked me. The realm of espionage fiction is full of government conspiracies and secrets, but they rarely occur in real life. But here, in a cold case dating to 1973, I discovered a tangled web of international espionage, vengeance, and multiple cover-ups by nations that should have known better. Researching the case took me from my middle-class neighborhood to the skies over North Vietnam, to the dark streets of downtown Beirut and the back alleys of Paris. The case was the ultimate onion: the more layers I peeled away, the more I found.

When I was promoted to deputy director of counterterrorism of the DSS, I tried to reopen the case formally. That turned out to be a lost cause. I was stonewalled at almost every turn.

During my years as a counterterrorism agent, I kept a black Moleskine book in my briefcase. In it I had listed the top international terrorists and unsolved cases that were my top priorities. When we caught or killed one of those on my list, I would scratch the name off and add a few notes on how and when justice was served.

After I left the DSS in the late 1990s to begin a second career as vice president for counterterrorism at Strategic Forecasting (Stratfor), I kept the black book close at hand. It represented unfinished business from my days in the field. Every now and then, one of those wanted criminals would be brought to justice, and I could cross another name off my list.

The perpetrators of the Bethesda crime remained unknown and at large. That I had not solved it remained an open wound from my DSS days. I needed closure—not just for myself now but for the Alon family, who had been victimized by the perpetrators. In the course of my investigation, I had formed a relationship with the family and had discovered just how poorly they had been treated by their own government. They needed to see justice served far more than I. In the counterterrorism business, we saw a lot of innocents whose suffering never abated. Justice proved elusive too many times. I did not want that to happen with this case.

I know a lot of other agents and cops who also work on cold cases into retirement. The unsolved ones are like unresolved elements of our own lives. They grow into obsessions, become part of us until we stake increasing amounts of our time, ego, and treasure on bringing the bad guys to justice. For years, my cold case dominated sections of our house in Austin, Texas. Initially, I covered the refrigerator in Post-it notes that linked one event or clue to another. When my family protested, I put a desk in the bedroom and transferred all my research there. The yellow sticky notes found their way to the wall in front of my coffee-stained desk. They served as the flowchart of the case; they were the way I traced its tentacles across time and space.

At night, after long days at Stratfor's Austin office, I would return home to spend time with the family. But when everyone else turned in, I would settle down and work on the case by the light of a Gerber tent lantern, so as not to awaken my wife. I followed old leads, pursued new ones, and developed a host of sources in unlikely locations.

Guilt propelled me forward. I should have done more on the case while with the DSS. I should have rattled enough cages at Langley to shake loose the files I needed. At the same time, being out of government service afforded me a level of freedom to maneuver that I would not have had otherwise. It allowed me to go off the grid and explore some dark corners of American diplomacy. It gave me the latitude to gradually unravel the multiple conspiracies that shrouded the motives and aftermath of that night in Bethesda.

The complexity of the case astonished me. The yellow sticky notes ultimately became the signposts of my journey across the decades. Whenever I got stuck, I would sit at the desk and let my eyes play across those notes: *Abu Iyad. A long-lost muscle car. Watergate. The Black Panthers. The MiG Menace. Professor X. The Suez Crisis. The Six-Day War.* The case was wrapped in a cocoon of disparate historic events, all of which came together in an unlikely confluence on a darkened street in my neighborhood in 1973. At times, the connections seemed overwhelming and the complexity impossible to grasp, which is why at the center of my Post-it notes

I placed a single name: Colonel Joe Alon. It was my way of staying grounded, a reminder that when I cut through that cocoon, what lay inside was a simple crime committed against an honorable and dedicated man. From that man and his rendezvous with fate one night in Bethesda, the case's investigative leads spread across the globe.

This book is the story of my three-decade pursuit of the truth behind what happened in my childhood hometown in the summer of 1973 and how the event helped shape international events for over a decade. At times the pursuit has been dangerous. Powerful and violent forces, both here and abroad, wanted the case to remain buried in the past. Some of my sources risked their lives to provide me with information. In return, within these pages I must protect their identities, lest even more blood be shed as a result of this case. Far too much has been shed already.

CHAPTER ONE
THE CRIME

Saturday, June 30, 1973

The summer of 1973 marked the first significant dividing line in my life. I was sixteen, about to start my junior year at Bethesda-Chevy Chase High School, and completely unprepared for the sudden dose of reality one episode of violence brought to my naive and limited view of the world.

Bethesda in the early 1970s was a safe haven, a place where nothing bad ever happened. Our neighbors in the sleepy, blue-collar bedroom community were the kind of people who built America and kept it great: factory workers, construction foremen, low-level government employees, cops, and firefighters. With brawn, reliability, and a can-do attitude, we were throwbacks to a different era. As the 1970s waned, ours became a dying breed.

My dad started out shoveling coal in West Virginia. After World War II, he tried his hand at building cars in Detroit. When that did not work out, he moved the family to Bethesda and opened up a gas station on the corner of Arlington Road and Bradley Boulevard.[1] The station is still there, a lone monument to an era long since consigned to yellowing newspapers and fading memories. In the intervening years, Bethesda has been Yuppified; it is the place where the D.C. gentry go to spawn.

My dad's Chevron station was only two blocks from our house. From the late 1960s throughout the 1970s, it was a sort of community center for my group of friends. In the mornings that summer, I would throw on a pair of jeans, an old white T-shirt, and a pair of tennis shoes, then run over to the station to start my day. I worked side by side with my old man, pumping gas, changing oil, and cleaning windshields as my pals dropped by to chat during the lulls in the business. Gas was twenty cents a gallon then, and nobody had heard of the Organization of Petroleum Exporting Countries (OPEC).

The gas station stood on a busy corner with a supermarket and hardware store across the street. In some ways, my father's gas station was the nexus for our little neighborhood. It was the one place everyone stopped at on their way to wherever their days took them. Some of Dad's customers included Spiro Agnew and other notable figures around D.C.

I often wonder if Joe Alon passed through our service islands. Had I ever filled his tank? I probably had, but I did not know him then. His '71 Galaxie 500 would have looked like anyone else's eight-cylinder sedan.

Looking back, that July ended up being the last good summer for us in Bethesda. The Yom Kippur War kicked off at the end of the summer. America's support of Israel during the war outraged the Arab world and triggered the OPEC oil embargo. In the midst of the oil crunch, the economy began a long downhill slide at same time Watergate unraveled the Nixon presidency.

I was about as politically aware as your average sixteen-year-old. The Vietnam War was a distant event I knew only through Walter Cronkite's broadcasts. The Apollo space program had ended the previous December, and there was not much else to hold a teenager's interest in the nightly WTOP radio news broadcasts I used to listen to in my dad's GMC truck. From my limited vantage point, it seemed we stood on the brink of a return to normalcy after all the turmoil the 1960s had brought. I was too young to understand that there was no going back. And I was too naive to recognize the brewing storm on the horizon.

That June 30 I spent the day pumping gas. At five, sunburned and oil-stained, Dad cut me loose, and I ran back home for a quick shower and a change of clothes. Cleaned up, I jumped in our 1965 GMC truck with an eight-track player and rolled out to meet my pals at The Tasty Diner, a fixture in Bethesda to this day.

If the gas station was the nexus for our neighborhood, Tasty's was the local hangout for high schoolers. It looked like an old Pullman railroad car stuck up on blocks in a weedy field. Inside, the double row of high-backed booths sported little jukeboxes arrayed on each table. We spent hours there, girl watching, listening to music, and discussing our one real passion: baseball.

Johnny Cash sang "Folsom Prison Blues" on the jukebox that evening when I arrived. The guys made room for me, and the waitress brought us burgers and Cokes. We decided to hit a movie later that night. The big summer release, *American Graffiti*, was a month away, but the trailers every week made us almost frantic to see it. The cars were too cool to miss.

———

Just south of my father's gas station was a maze of residential roads. In the middle of this little enclave stretched Trent Street.

Shortly after sunset, while we kids went about our summer routine, Joe Alon and his wife, Dvora, returned to their Trent Street home after a day and evening of shopping.[2] Their oldest daughter, Dalia, who was a senior with us at B-CC High, had been gone all day on a first date with a boy she had met at the Roy Rogers where she worked as a waitress. The Alons' other two daughters, Yola, fourteen, and Rachel, six, had stayed at home all day. When the Alons returned that evening, they found Yola and Rachel curled up in the living room watching television.

Joe and Dvora had been invited to a party earlier that week, and the day before Joe had confirmed his attendance. Now, at nine-thirty that evening, Joe put on a pair of brown slacks, a white shirt and tie with a gold tie clasp, and a red sport coat. His wife slipped into a cocktail dress. Joe escorted Dvora out to the Ford Galaxie 500 sedan sitting in the driveway. Before they left, someone switched on the porch lights, bathing the front yard in their amber glow. The garage door stood open, which was not unusual. Crime was nonexistent back then in Bethesda. Hardly anyone bothered to lock their doors. It was a Saturday night, and a party waited up on East Kirk Street, a few miles away. Even though he should have been watching his back, he felt that security was not an issue.

Not long after Joe and his wife drove away for the party, a shadow crossed the front yard. A man, moving with speed and stealth, stole across the driveway and slipped behind some bushes that flanked the garage. The figure waited with discipline and patience. Inside the house, their girls fell asleep in front of the television.

Three hours passed. Dalia and her date, Robert Dempsey, drove up Trent Street in his light blue VW Bug. He walked her to the porch, said good night, and left without going inside. Dalia locked the front door behind her once she was inside the house. Her arrival woke up Rachel and Yola, who shut off the TV and went to bed. Within minutes, the house was totally dark. Only the porch lights remained on.

Outside, the figure remained still and hidden behind the bushes near the garage. The three girls inside were at their most vulnerable, tucked away in their beds, back door unlocked, garage wide open. But the figure was not interested in the girls. He continued his vigil from the bushes, eyes scanning for the return of the family's Ford sedan.

At twelve-thirty, Joe and Dvora left the party on East Kirk Street. Joe insisted on driving, although he had been drinking throughout the evening. He slid behind the wheel while Dvora snuggled close to him on the bench seat. Cautiously, he puttered home to the one-story rambler on Trent Street. Just before 1:00 A.M., the green Ford rolled to a stop on the driveway in front of the garage. The porch lights no longer blazed, and when Joe shut off the sedan's headlights, darkness cloaked the yard. Unconcerned, Dvora popped out of the passenger's side of the car and headed for the front door without waiting for her husband. Joe, who had left his red sport coat in the backseat, opened his door, stepped out, then leaned inside to retrieve the coat. With his back to the yard, bent over awkwardly, Joe never saw the figure slip from bushes and walk toward him.

Dvora had just opened the front door when she heard the first shot. Glancing back, she saw her husband stagger by the car. She ran inside as four more shots rang out. The daughters, roused by the noise, poured into the living room. Dvora went through the kitchen, opened the door to the garage, and flicked on the light, hoping to see her husband. She could not see him. Up the street, a car's headlights shined to life, catching Dvora's attention. It rolled past the Alon house, and she could see it was a white, full-size sedan. It drove off down Trent Street and vanished into the night. She had never seen that car in the neighborhood before.

Suddenly, a thought occurred to her. The garage light had illuminated the driveway. If the gunman was still out there, it would make Joe an easier target. Dvora herself was an easy target now, standing in the doorway at the back of the garage. Quickly, she flicked the light off, closed the door, and dialed the Montgomery County Police.

The operator wanted so much information that Dvora was overwhelmed. She handed the phone to Yola, grabbed some towels, and told Dalia to follow her. Going through the front door, they ran out into the night in search of their husband and father.

They found Joe on his back in the grass beside the driveway. Blood was everywhere. Dvora and Dalia fell to their knees and went to work, desperately trying to staunch the bleeding. But there were too many wounds. Joe tried to speak, but no words came out. Dvora held his head while Dalia placed the towels across his chest. An ambulance from the Bethesda-Chevy Chase Rescue Squad roared up Trent Street. The paramedics arrived to find both mother and daughter splattered with blood, Joe's body still in Dvora's arms.[3]

Traumatized and reeling, Dvora rode in the ambulance with Joe's body as it drove to Suburban Hospital. Back at the Trent Street house, the Montgomery County Police descended on the crime scene, searching for clues. Somewhere in the night, a killer remained at large.

———————

The next morning, I awoke to the news that there had been a murder in our neighborhood. The *Washington Post*, which ran a front-page story, gave only the basics of the crime.[4] I read the article over breakfast, stunned that one of my schoolmates could be touched by such raw violence. Was it a random street crime? Was it something more? If it was something more, then who was Joe Alon and why would anyone want him dead? I think many people in Bethesda were asking those same questions around their breakfast tables that morning.

Twenty-four hours after the murder, Dvora and her daughters boarded Air Force Two (part of the presidential air fleet used to back up Air Force One) and flew to Israel.[5] No one saw two of the daughters again until 2010, when we met at the house with an Israeli TV crew to discuss the murder.

CHAPTER TWO
THE LION OF HATZOR

1920s–1960s

Joseph Alon lived in an average American neighborhood in an average-size house and drove a nondescript American sedan.[1] His children attended the local public schools, just like most everyone else in Bethesda at that time. At first glance, there seemed to be no reason behind Joe's murder. It seemed random and disturbingly out of place for our community.

The fact was, the image Joe portrayed was carefully cultivated and concealed his true identity, which was anything but ordinary.

For starters, Joe Alon was not an American, and his real name was not Joe Alon.[2]

————

In the 1920s, Joe's Zionist parents emigrated from Brno, in what was then Czechoslovakia, to Palestine, where they settled on a kibbutz in the Jezreel Valley near Mount Gilboa. When Joseph was born in 1929, his last name was Placzek. Two years later, his family was driven off the kibbutz by ongoing Arab-Jewish violence and returned to Brno. The Placzeks were a well-known and re-spected Jewish family there and no doubt were welcomed back. Joe's father, Friedrich, had a brother named Georg who was a noted physicist. Prior to World War II, Georg emigrated to the United States, where he taught at Princeton and later joined the Manhattan Project.

In 1939, just before the German invasion of Czechoslovakia, Joe's father sent his ten-year-old son to live in England. He had the foresight to see what fate held for his country and his people. Joe got out just in time, though his brother and sister remained in Brno.

In March of that year, the Germans swept into Prague, the Czech capital. Eight days after the invasion, German soldiers murdered Friedrich Placzek. Two years later, the Nazis rounded up most of the Czech Jews—Joe's mother and sister among them—and moved them into the Terezin Ghetto, which had been established inside a series of eighteenth-century fortresses. The ghetto later became known as Theresienstadt concentration camp. The inmates, who ultimately numbered almost 150,000, were forced to serve as slave laborers for the Third Reich, man-ufacturing coffins, sorting confiscated Jewish clothing that was shipped to Germans who had been bombed out of their homes by the Royal Air Force, and splitting locally mined mica. The con-ditions were cramped and squalid, leading to outbreaks of typhus and other diseases. Malnutrition claimed thousands of lives, as the Germans kept the Jews on starvation rations or worse. Tor-ture and random murders were part of everyday life at Terezin.

In June 1944, the Germans allowed the International Red Cross to visit the camp. In preparation for that visit, Terezin re-ceived a propaganda makeover designed to convince the Red

Cross that conditions were not only humane but luxurious. Faux stores were created within the fortress and stocked liberally with imported goods, food, and consumer items. Washrooms were constructed, and the Jewish inmates were given better clothing and told to behave. The window-dressing paid off. The Red Cross reported there were no problems at Theresienstadt. A propaganda movie was made, using a Jewish director and Jewish inmates for actors, that showed how well and humanely the camp functioned.

A few months later, the Germans shipped two-thirds of the Theresienstadt inmates to Auschwitz, including Joe's mother and sister, where they were all murdered. The director and all of the actors who took part in the propaganda film were among those slain.

By the time the Soviet Red Army reached Theresienstadt in May 1945, only 17,250 starving and disease-wracked Jews remained alive. Of the 15,000 children sent to the ghetto and camp, fewer than 100 lived to see the Soviets liberate the camp.

Joe Placzek survived the war, thanks to his father's foresight and decision to send him abroad. In England, Joe watched the war unfold. He studied in English schools, learned the language, and thrived despite his separation from his family. His parents, brother, and sister were never far from his mind. After the war ended, he traveled back to Brno, where he discovered that the Nazis had virtually annihilated his community and family.

He learned first of his father's death, then that his mother and sister had survived the hell of the Terezin Ghetto only to be gassed at Auschwitz, most likely in a mass extermination in the fall of 1944. Only his brother, his uncle Georg the Princeton professor, and another uncle survived the war.

———————

At first, Joe tried to settle down in Brno and learn a trade. He decided to become a jeweler, but that did not last. As he reached manhood, Europe's surviving Jews fled the Old World for the hope of a new nation in Palestine. Fighting between these Jews and the Palestinian Arabs raged throughout 1946 and 1947. The British found themselves caught in the middle, alternating between trying to suppress the Jewish resistance and mediating between the Jews and Arabs. Neither approach worked.

After all their suffering in Europe, the Jews wanted to return to their original homeland—they wanted their own nation again. The last remnants of the Jewish people saw this as their only hope. Hitler had almost wiped them out. Now they would make their stand and fight for independence.

The resistance, called the Haganah (the "Defense"), needed weapons, and lots of them. Wealthy Jewish donors, including many Americans, funneled money to the Palestinian Jews so that they could purchase machine guns, rifles, and ammunition. Most nations refused to sell arms to the Jews, but the Czech government obliged. Starting in June 1947, the Czechs sold the Haganah some 35,000 leftover German rifles and 5,500 machine guns. The Jewish underground in Europe smuggled these weapons past the British blockade of Palestine to get them to the desperate resistance fighters.

The weapon sales proved to be the springboard for further Czech support. Male and female Jews eager to join the fight made their way to Czechoslovakia, where they formed an infantry brigade. The Czechs armed the unit and provided extensive training. The effort solidified the relationship between Israel and

Czechoslovakia and led to even more military support in the months to come.

In 1948, with most of his family dead and his people in peril once again, Joe Placzek abandoned his peaceful jeweler's life and joined the Jewish underground in Czechoslovakia. That spring, the Jews declared the establishment of the State of Israel. The pronouncement sent shock waves across the world and triggered a war in the Middle East. Attacked by Jordan, Syria, Egypt, and Iraq, the nascent Jewish state faced extinction. More than anything, the Israelis needed an air force to protect its cities and military bases. The Haganah had flown some light aircraft—basically Piper Cubs equipped with hand grenades and rifles—but the Israelis lacked modern combat aircraft and the pilots to fly them.

A call for volunteers rang out. From all over the world—South Africa, England, Canada, the United States, Australia, and Europe—veteran Jewish pilots who had served in World War II stepped forward to help defend Israel. Simultaneously, Israeli agents scoured the world for any aircraft they could purchase and throw into their fight for independence. In the United States, several Israeli agents managed to purchase four-engine B-17 Flying Fortress heavy bombers through a dummy corporation. Just as the federal government grew suspicious, the planes were flown out of the country and made their way to Israel, where the air force used them to attack Egyptian and Syrian targets.

More aircraft flowed into Israel from war-surplus stocks in Europe. At the same time, the Arab nations were busily scouring the world for combat aircraft of their own. Some of the first planes they got came from the United Kingdom: the Egyptians negotiated a deal with the British for some Spitfire fighters. The

Haganah's misfit band of pilots and smuggled aircraft would be no match for these high-performance planes. The Spitfires threatened to turn the growing war in the air decisively against the Israelis. Lose the air war, lose the war. The Israelis had to find something that could defeat the new Egyptian menace.

Again the Israelis turned to Czechoslovakia for help. The Prague government agreed to sell Israel almost a hundred World War II–era fighter planes. Ironically, the planes were homegrown versions of the legendary German Messerschmitt Bf-109, the Spitfire's World War II archadversary.

The Czechs also agreed to establish a secret operation to train eighty-five pilots to fly the new fighters. At age nineteen, Joe Placzek stepped forward and volunteered to fly in defense of his people. He and others began their flight training in the summer of 1948. Meanwhile, Israel battled for its life on multiple fronts. Joe could not wait to get into the fight. The pilots were sorely needed, and they knew it.

Not long after their aerial training began, Soviet dictator Joseph Stalin intervened to end this operation in support of Israel. Not wanting to see the Jews achieve dominance over the Arab enemies, he ordered the communist Czech government to cease all military aid to Israel. The training stopped, and the supply of arms and aircraft dried up. The pilots and soldiers of the volunteer brigade left Czechoslovakia and found their way to Israel. Joe Placzek arrived with this wave of armed and dedicated volunteers in the fall of 1948. In Israel, Placzek changed his name to Joseph Alon, shedding his old name as he made a new start with his fellow survivors of the Holocaust.

His time learning to fly in Prague was not wasted. The Israel Defense Forces ordered Joe to join its very first flight class, which graduated in 1949. By the time he received his wings, the ragtag band of volunteers had helped beat back the Arab menace. Israel prevailed, but the seeds for three more wars had been sown.

———————

As a child, Joe's family had fled the Middle East to escape war, only to be consumed in the Shoah in the 1940s. With his parents and grandparents dead, Joe had led a rootless existence ever since he had been sent to England. At last, in the fledgling Israeli Air Force (IAF), Joe found his place in the world. Flying became his life. It consumed him; he loved the freedom the skies offered. Perhaps in the wild blue, he found answers to questions that surely dogged him. At least, he found meaning. From his humble aspirations to be a jeweler, he would become a protector of his people, a pilot of rare abilities, and an officer with the charisma and intellect needed to get men to follow him willingly into battle, no matter how long the odds.

The young pilot's superiors noticed his ability right away. They sent him to jet fighter school, and he emerged in the early 1950s as one of Israel's first jet fighter pilots. Originally, he flew British-made Gloster Meteor fighter jets. These aircraft, which had first seen service at the end of World War II, had quickly become obsolete. The Meteor was first generation, long since surpassed by more modern designs entering service in the 1950s. Nevertheless, the Israelis used the Gloster as an all-weather day-and-night interceptor. Joe and his fellow Meteor pilots had one key mission: defend Israel's cities from Egypt's bomber fleet. Only a handful of expert pilots were ever trusted with that vital role.

In the mid-1950s, Israel stood as a tiny oasis, surrounded by hostile nations. The Arab coalition that had tried to crush the Jewish state in the 1948–1949 war continued in their hope that they would eventually prevail. Indeed, Syria and Egypt spent the early and mid-1950s buying as many airplanes, tanks, and artillery pieces as they could find and afford. Ironically, now Egypt found a willing seller in Czechoslovakia. By early 1956, the Czechs provided the Egyptian Air Force with some of the best Soviet-made aircraft of the era, including the stubby MiG-15 Fagot, the legendary swept-wing fighter that had caused the U.S. Air Force so much trouble over Korea.

Israel faced an arms race it could not win. Not only did it not have the money to match the Egyptian and Syrian buildup plane for plane, but it still had trouble getting anyone to sell it the equipment it needed for survival.

Then the French stepped in and offered their latest-generation fighters and tanks. Whatever the Israelis could pay for, they could have. The IAF ended up buying the swept-wing Mystère IV fighter to counter Egypt's MiG threat. To supplement the Mystère, which was inferior to the MiG in almost every way but still much better than the decade-old Meteors and war-weary prop-driven aircraft then in Israeli service, the IAF purchased a squadron's worth of Dassault Ouragan fighter-bombers.

In 1955, the IAF entrusted Joe Alon with this vital core of jet aircraft. He took command of Number 113 Squadron and taught a whole generation of Israeli pilots to fly the Ouragan. It was not the best fighter plane. It was not the fastest. But it did have four cannon and could carry sixteen unguided rockets. As an attack jet tasked with supporting troops and blasting enemy vehicles on their way to the front lines, it fit the bill nicely.

Alon forged a tight-knit group in 113 Squadron. The men would have followed him anywhere. His ease of spirit, his casual grin, and his great sense of humor meshed perfectly with a can-do spirit that never dimmed. When presented with obstacles, he always found a way to get what his men needed. During their off hours, Joe frequently invited his pilots over for dinner. His wife, Dvora, whom he married in January 1954, became known for her delicious meals. At one time or another, most of Israel's combat pilots passed through the Alon dining room.

In October 1956, war broke out between Israel and Egypt. The countries were prodded into the war by France and Britain, which were enraged that Egypt's president, Gamal Abdel Nasser, had nationalized the Suez Canal. Although the war lasted only a few weeks before a cease-fire went into effect, those few weeks saw intense combat operations that centered on an Israeli drive into the Sinai. At the start of the war, the IAF, using thirty-year-old transport planes, dropped a force of crack paratroopers, led by future–prime minister Ariel Sharon, deep behind Egyptian lines. Their job was to seize and hold a key strategic point known as the Mitla Pass, which served as the gateway to the central Sinai.

The paratroopers ran into brutal and effective resistance. The Egyptians refused to give ground, and the battle raged along the pass's steep cliffs. At times, the Israelis found themselves fighting cave to cave, clearing diehard Egyptians out with hand grenades.

The Egyptians threw in their reserves. Reinforced with artillery and tanks, the forces defending Mitla Pass gained the upper hand. Sharon's paratroopers suffered heavy losses and were threatened with annihilation.

The Israelis turned to their air force, hoping the new jets could save the men on the ground. It was a tough mission, made more complicated by the fact that Israel had exactly two dozen Mystère IV fighters to fend off over a hundred Czech-provided MiG-15s. Besides a few squadrons of ancient, World War II–era

P-51 Mustang prop planes, only Joe Alon's twenty Ouragans had the capability to carry out these difficult ground-attack missions.

Without their intervention, the paratroops surely would have died. Joe's men strapped into their French jets and took to the skies. The first missions ran into a buzz saw of MiG-15s. Dogfights raged overhead, even as the Egyptians brought up more men, tanks, and guns. The war hung in the balance. Running low over the rugged terrain, the Ouragans waded into the fray.

On the first day of the war, Joe led two of his squadron's Ouragans to the Mitla Pass. Overhead, Mystères engaged the Egyptian MiGs ranging over the battlefield. Freed from the threat of aerial interception, he and his wingman strafed, rocketed, and destroyed a 130mm mortar battery that had been causing many casualties among the paratroops.

The next day, the Lions of Hatzor, as 113 Squadron was known, flew over ten missions against the Egyptians at Mitla Pass. Several times, MiG-15s dove down on them from above, cannon blazing. The Ouragan was a straight-wing jet, an older and slower design than the swept-back MiGs. The Lions could not outclimb, outrun, or even outturn the Egyptian fighters. All they could do was outfight them. In the months before the war, Joe Alon had trained his men to be hyperaggressive. If outnumbered, fight like banshees. Never give up, and always attack. To emphasize that aggression, he had every Ouragan in the squadron painted with a ferocious-looking shark's mouth, complete with yawning grin and razor-sharp teeth. The planes looked formidable, and the pilots backed the image up.

That spirit paid off in October. When MiGs attacked 113 Squadron on the second day of the war, Alon's pilots parried their moves, turned their guns on the flashing brown and green Egyptian fighters, and prevailed through sheer superior tactics and skill. The squadron did not lose a single Ouragan to enemy fighters—a miraculous achievement considering how out-matched its planes were.

Thanks to the close air support the Lions provided, the para-troops cleared and held Mitla Pass, allowing follow-up brigades of infantry and armor to pour into the Sinai Peninsula and drive all the way to the Suez Canal. Mission accomplished. When the war ended, Joe Alon's squadron of ground-attack specialists played the leading role in the destruction of almost 350 tanks, halftracks, and other armored vehicles: almost a quarter of all the fighting vehicles Egypt had deployed into the Sinai. The stun-ning victory made the IDF leadership true believers in close co-operation between the army and air force.

The war and the Lions' success confirmed Joe Alon as one of the best tactical-level officers in the IAF. Promotions followed. In four years, Joe was a lieutenant colonel, entrusted with bring-ing Israel's first Mach 2 fighter, the French Dassault Mirage III delta-winged fighter-bomber, into front-line service.

After the 1956 war, Egypt and Syria continued to expand their air forces, thanks to easily available Soviet equipment. The MiG-15s gave way to the newer MiG-17s, then MiG-19s and the ultra-fast, very capable MiG-21 interceptors. Once again, the Israelis found themselves in an arms race they simply could not win. They had neither the money nor the manpower to match the Syrian and Egyptian buildups. Instead, the IAF focused on two things: buying the best available fighter in the world and matching it with the best-trained, most dedicated, and hardest-core pilots in the world.

To carry out this task, the air force turned to Joe Alon. Joe was more than up to the job, even though the Mirage III repre-sented a quantum technological leap from everything then in service with the IAF. The delta-winged configuration made its controls ultra-sensitive, a fact that Joe discovered on his first flight. As he lifted off from the runway, observers saw the Mirage's nose suddenly tilt sharply skyward. Joe fought the controls and overcorrected. The big fighter's nose plunged earthward. He pulled out of the dive at the last second before the Mirage plowed into the ground. As he leveled off, he was so low that the jet's exhaust blew up a storm of dirt, sand, and dust in its wake.

A lesser pilot would not have survived, but that was why Joe flew the plane first. He learned the Mirage's quirks, figured out how best to fly it, then shared that information with the crack group of pilots assembled and ready to take it into service. The Mirage III became the backbone of Israel's air superiority fighter strength, the aircraft that would rule Middle East skies for almost a decade. Joe Alon laid the foundation for that superiority as the commander of the first Mirage squadron, Number 101.

———————

The 1960s saw a steady increase in tension between Israel and its neighbors. By 1967, the Middle East had heated to a boiling point. This time, on the eve of war, Joe Alon had been promoted to full colonel and given command of the first air base built from the ground up by the IAF; its other bases had all been holdovers from the British-mandate era of the 1920s, 1930s, and 1940s. It was here that Joe played another key role in the structure and function of the IAF.

By 1965, the Egyptian Air Force had grown so large that the Israelis realized that, in the event of war, even with their superior pilots and high-tech Mirage IIIs, they stood a real chance of being overwhelmed by sheer numbers. Worse, chances were high that should a conflict come, Israel would be fighting on three fronts:

north against Syria and Iraq, east against Jordan, and south against Egypt.

The IAF had to be larger in the air than it was on the ground. With fewer than a hundred Mirage IIIs for air defense, the IAF calculated that its very survival depended on how fast these aircraft could be landed, refueled, rearmed, and sent back out on another mission. Increasing the number of sorties per aircraft during a conflict might go a long way in leveling the odds.

Alon's base became a test case for this hypothesis. He helped reorganize the way ground crews prepared their planes for battle. No longer would a plane be parked after a mission and left in a revetment to be refueled and rearmed by mobile trucks and crews. Instead, the IAF adopted Henry Ford's mass production model. The returning aircraft would move from one station to the next, getting fuel, ammunition, minor repairs, rockets, bombs, and fuel tanks placed on pylons under the wings. The pilots would not even get out of their cockpits. They would simply steer through the stations, then swing back out on the runway as they received their mission briefing over the radio.

It was a brilliant and elegant solution to the IAF's numerical inferiority. The new model worked so well that the sortie rate skyrocketed. Although the pilots and crews suffered from extreme fatigue at full tempo, the birds always got in the air.

Still, IAF planners realized that even this might not be enough to tip the scales in Israel's favor. They concluded that the only way to gain air superiority in the event of war was to strike first, using the element of surprise to destroy enemy air forces on the ground. Do that, and the Mirages could patrol the skies while the ground-attack fighters attacked Arab tanks and supply trucks.

That is exactly what happened in 1967. That June, after months of tension, the Egyptians blockaded Israel's only port on the Red Sea. War broke out soon after. This time the Israelis struck first, just as their planners had wanted. The air force delivered knockout blows to both the Egyptians and Syrians. Hundreds of brand-new MiG fighters and Tupolev bombers went up in flames without ever lifting off a runway. When the dust settled six days later, Israel controlled the West Bank and the critical Golan Heights to the north and had achieved complete air supremacy over four well-armed and equipped nations. It was a feat unique in history. The war inflicted a permanent and lasting sense of global humiliation on the Arab nations that proved so profound that it recast the order of the Middle East and laid the foundation for decades of terrorism.

Joe Alon spent the Six-Day War in command of Israel's flight training base. That did not stop him from flying in combat, however. When war came, the IAF threw every able-bodied pilot and aircraft into the fray. Even flight instructors and cadets were expected to fly combat missions in their Fouga Magister light training jets. In fact, just before the war started, some forty-four Magisters were redeployed to operational bases. While the Mirage IIIs and Ouragans went after the Egyptian and Syrian air forces, the Magisters served as close air support platforms. During the war's opening days, Alon and his instructors and cadets flung themselves into Arab antiaircraft fire while they attacked armored vehicles in the Sinai. These jets, nominally combat capable, took heavy losses. In one mission, four Fougas were lost to enemy fire.

On the second day of the war, Joe's trainers-turned-warriors faced off against a massive Jordanian armored counterattack directed at the Israeli troops fighting around Jerusalem. The Fougas came whistling low over the battlefield, rockets sizzling off their rails. One after another, Jordanian tanks exploded in flames. Although they faced intense antiaircraft fire, the Magister pilots flew with near-suicidal bravery. When they pulled off target, 120 armored vehicles lay smashed and burning. It was a key moment, one that probably saved the Israeli effort on the West Bank.

In the four remaining days of the war, Joe's pilots turned their wrath against the Syrians on the Golan Heights. Once again, their fragile, vulnerable little jets came under heavy fire. Planes went down and pilots died. But the cadets and instructors never let up the pace. When the war ended, seven of Joe's Fougas had been shot down, and six pilots had been killed.

In the months after the Six-Day War, Colonel Joseph Alon could look back on almost twenty years of devoted service to his nation. He had graduated in the air force's founding flight class, fought in two wars, helped modernize the IAF twice, led two elite squadrons, and played an important role in creating the ultra-fast turnaround times that allowed the Israelis to fly more sorties than any other air force in the world. He was a legend in the IAF and a national hero, a man who embodied the resolve and courage that carried Israel through every crisis since its inception.

But what was an Israeli war hero doing in my Bethesda neighborhood in 1973?

CHAPTER THREE
THE INVESTIGATION BEGINS

July 1973

The ambulance sped away from the Trent Street house carrying Joe Alon and his sobbing wife.[1] At Suburban Hospital, the physician on call, Dr. Janos Tibor Bacsanyi, pronounced Joe dead at 1:27 A.M.[2]

Covered in her husband's blood, Dvora remained at the hospital while calls were made to the medical examiner to arrange an autopsy. The Montgomery County Medical Examiner, Dr. Ball, ordered Joe's body to be sent to Baltimore, where a better-equipped facility was available.

Sergeant William McKee, an officer with the Montgomery County Police Department (MCPD) assigned to the robbery section, had been one of the first to respond to Dvora's emergency call. After a short time on the scene, he sped to the hospital, where he found Dvora and began to interview her. He had asked only a few preliminary questions when two members of the Israeli embassy arrived and interrupted them. They took Dvora and the girls to the embassy, where they spent much of the remainder of the night.

Without a witness to interview, Sergeant McKee looked for Joe's personal effects. In his pocket, McKee found a wallet containing a permit for a .38 caliber pistol and sixty-two dollars in cash. Clearly, robbery was not a motive for the murder that night.

Back at the Trent Street house, the MCPD began to examine the crime scene. As they worked, the Israeli military attaché, Major General Mordechai Gur, drove up and introduced himself. General Gur was a legend in the Israeli military, having served in Ariel Sharon's paratrooper unit during the 1956 war, then spearheading the assault that wrested Jerusalem away from the Jordanians in 1967's Six-Day War. His paratroopers were photographed in tears at the Wailing Wall, an image that became an iconic symbol to the Israeli people, akin to the famous flag-raising photo taken on Iwo Jima during World War II.

General Gur spoke with the police officers on the scene and told them he was not aware of any threats against Joe or his family and that there had been no indications that any members of the embassy staff were in danger. The general had been at the party Joe and Dvora had attended earlier in the evening, and nothing had seemed unusual or noteworthy there either.

General Gur remained on the scene, and Dvora returned home from the embassy. When he saw her, Dvora later recalled that General Gur cried out that he wished it had been he who had been shot, not Joe.

The official police report revealed an important detail regarding General Gur. During their interview, General Gur assured the officers that Joe Alon was not involved in any type of intelligence operations.[3] Gur would later contradict his original statement in a subsequent discussion.

According to the police report, when Dvora returned home, the MCPD officers finally were able to interview her. By this time she must have been numb with shock and grief. Her husband was dead, her family was shattered, and she had had no sleep or time to think. Nevertheless, she walked the police through the evening, detailing how she had heard the gunshots, called for help, and seen a white sedan drive slowly up Trent Street.

The officers asked her if anything unusual had happened in the weeks prior to the murder. She remembered nothing out of the ordinary: no unusual visitors and no conversations with Joe that would lead her to think there had been threats against him.

As they spoke, the Federal Bureau of Investigation arrived. The MCPD locals had called Stanley Orenstein, an agent assigned to the Silver Spring, Maryland, FBI office.[4] From his home, he made a few phone calls to begin the FBI's involvement in the case.[5]

The FBI agents who showed up that night let the MCPD officers continue their witness interviews. Dalia had been getting ready for bed after getting home from her date with Robert Dempsey when the shots rang out. She had not seen anything unusual, although, when asked, she vaguely recalled that a white sedan may have been parked across the street from their house.

It was not much to go on, but the investigators combed the crime scene looking for additional evidence. At noon on July 1, the autopsy on Joe was performed. It took only an hour to complete. The assistant medical examiner, Dr. Ronald Kornblum, began by taking hair samples, finger- and palm prints, and X-rays, which showed that no bullets had remained lodged in Joe's body. This meant that there would be evidence left at the scene. Dr. Kornblum also performed a neutron activation test on Joe's hands for gunpowder residue. The test proved conclusively that Joe had not fired a weapon that night. Even if he had been armed, he would have had no time to react to his assailant.[6]

The autopsy revealed two bullet wounds in Joe's right wrist and hand. Three more bullets had struck him in the chest. Two of those bullets had inflicted grazing wounds that passed across him left to right, suggesting he was in left profile to his murderer. Neither had entered his body cavity, and both would have been survivable.

The fatal shot had struck Joe under his left arm, continued through his heart, and exited through the right side of his chest.[7] Hitting a man in the heart from eight to twelve feet away with a .38 caliber pistol in the dead of night was either a lucky fluke or the work of a skilled marksman.

After the autopsy was finished, Alon's body and his family departed for Israel, leaving the FBI and the MCPD without access to their only witnesses.[8]

Still, work on the scene continued. The MCPD and FBI worked together and located two of the five bullets fired on the night of the murder. The first was found on the ground not far from the left door of the Alons' Galaxie 500. After digging around in the front seat, the investigators located fragments of a second bullet. The one on the ground yielded the best forensic evidence yet. It was a .38 caliber, copper-jacketed, military-style round.

A search of the house quickly located Joe's .38 in the bedroom. The gun was sent to the FBI lab in Washington, D.C., for further testing, along with the two recovered bullets, to determine whether the shots had been fired from Alon's own pistol. Whenever a homicide occurs, the police want to rule out whether or not the victim's own gun was used by either a family member or another suspect. Routine procedure is to test the guns owned by the victim with the wounds. The FBI lab quickly returned with a verdict. Joe's revolver was not the murder weapon. This eliminated Dvora and her daughters as potential suspects, and most likely removed passion or a domestic dispute as motives.

While waiting for the test results, the MCPD sent a team of officers from the homicide squad to rake the crime scene for more evidence. The police set up a grid on the Alons' front yard to organize their search for clues; each square of the grid was searched painstakingly for days. The team then worked through the neighborhood in search of the remaining three bullets. When that failed, the FBI used a metal detector to search the area. Despite their best efforts, however, the remaining three bullets were never found.

Five days after the murder, the FBI and the MCPD gathered at the crime scene again with Dr. Kornblum to reconstruct what had happened that night. Based on the entry wounds, Joe's location when he was hit, plus the bullet damage to the Alons' Ford, the reconstruction concluded that the murderer had fired from behind an evergreen tree directly to the left of the garage. After examining the scene and the bullet trajectories, Dr. Kornblum estimated the height of the murderer to be between five-foot-seven and six feet.

A search behind the evergreen tree revealed a number of cigarette butts. Chances were good that they belonged to the killer, who must have been stationed there for some time before Joe and his wife returned home. To pass the time, he smoked. The Montgomery County investigators carefully bagged and tagged the butts. The butts and all the remaining evidence, including Joe's wallet, were turned over to FBI Special Agent Frank Korn, who had been assigned to the case from the Silver Spring office. The fact that the FBI took custody over all the physical evidence in the case would have profound consequences later.

At this point, the MCPD focused on potential local suspects to determine if Joe's death was the result of some sort of street crime. Both the sex squad and the robbery squad drafted lists of known incidents and felons who had worked in the Trent Street neighborhood or had ties to it. The sex squad searched back to January 1973 while the robbery squad focused on property thefts, muggings, and burglaries over the previous few months. Together, they came up with over eighteen suspects. The list, along with mug shots and background information, was then turned over to the FBI office in Silver Spring on the night of the murder.

The FBI took a broader approach to the investigation. Its agents checked with all the local rental car companies in search of the white sedan. That took weeks, and they came up empty-handed. They checked the local airports to see if anyone suspicious had flown out of the country after the murder. Again they drew a blank.[9]

Both departments tried to find additional witnesses. Agents and officers went door to door through the Trent Street neighborhood, hoping to find someone who had seen the white sedan or anything else suspicious. That proved to be another dead end. They interviewed everyone who attended the party Joe and Dvora had been at before the murder. That yielded one tantalizing clue: a couple of partygoers remembered seeing a mid-1960s blue sedan with four olive-skinned male occupants parked near the scene. The investigators never located the car or its occupants.

Dalia's date that evening, Robert Dempsey, was interviewed on July 2, 1973. He told an FBI agent that he was particularly nervous bringing Dalia home due to the late hour. He had parked in front of the house and walked her to the front door to say good-bye. The FBI agent asked if he had entered the house. He replied that he had not because he was afraid that the Alons would be upset with him for keeping their daughter out after midnight. So he beat a hasty retreat to his car and drove back to his home in Manassas, Virginia.

The FBI agent asked if he had seen anything unusual on Trent Street that night. Dempsey replied all seemed normal. Most important to the police, when he reached the Alon house, he turned around and parked across the street before getting out and escorting Dalia to the front door. He saw no white sedan, and he was certain there were no other cars parked near the Alon house when he was there. He left between 12:20 and 12:30 that morning.

Joe and Dvora had left the party sometime after 12:30, arriving home about 1:00 A.M. If Dempsey's recollections were correct—and he was far more sure of the hour than Dalia was—the white sedan showed up on Trent Street sometime *after* the Alons headed home. It had not been waiting for them, a fact that strongly suggested that some sort of surveillance operation was following Joe. It also pointed to a conspiracy that involved at the very least the killer, the driver of the white sedan, and possibly four more men in the blue car seen near the location of the party. If all these pieces fit together, the conspirators would have needed to communicate with each other, something easier said than done in an age before cell phones and effective handheld radios.

The pursuit of Joe's killer never really gained any traction. What leads the FBI and MCPD developed all resulted in dead ends. Both agencies expended tremendous numbers of man-hours with little result. At best, all the work undertaken served merely to eliminate potential motives and suspects.

The killer and his accomplices had slipped away in those early-morning hours of July 1, 1973, vanishing without a trace.

CHAPTER FOUR
DVORA'S QUEST

Summer and Fall 1973

Dvora returned home to Israel with her daughters on July 3, 1973.[1] According to Jewish tradition, a body should not be tampered with after death, so embalming is prohibited. Instead, the body is supposed to be returned to the creator as quickly as possible. As a result, Colonel Joseph Alon was buried right after his family arrived in Israel. He was laid to rest in an unremarkable wooden coffin and given a hero's funeral.[2]

A few days later, Dvora hosted a gathering of family friends at her home outside of Tel Aviv. Besides Joe's fellow fighter pilots, the attendees that evening included a who's-who of Israel's civilian and military leadership, including Ezer Weizman, one of the founding members of the Israeli Air Force and the nephew of Israel's first president, Professor Chaim Weizman. Ezer had learned to fly in the British Royal Air Force during World War II after enlisting at age eighteen. During Israel's struggle for independence, he had flown a Spitfire during some of the IAF's first aerial engagements. Later, when he became the commander of the air force in 1958, he located his old Spitfire, painted it black with slashing horizontal stripes on either side of the fuselage, and used it as his personal aircraft for years. After serving as deputy chief of staff for the Israel Defense Forces (IDF), he retired in 1969 as a major general. Subsequently, Weizman entered the political arena. In 1993, he served as Israel's seventh president, resigning in 2000 after a financial scandal.

General Moshe Dayan also came to the memorial that evening, which ended up causing a minor scene. He had served with the British army during World War II, where he had lost an eye to a Vichy French bullet while scouting a river crossing in Lebanon in 1941. For the rest of his life, he wore a black eye patch that ultimately became his trademark—as recognizable to Israeli soldiers as Patton's ivory-handled pistols were to American soldiers.

After leading a tank unit in the War of Independence, Dayan served as the IDF's chief of staff during the 1950s. When he retired in 1959, he joined the Israeli Labor Party and later served as foreign minister and defense minister in various cabinets. By 1973, he and Weizman—two old comrades in arms—had become political opponents, as Weizman had joined the conservative, right-wing party.

The night of Joseph Alon's memorial, Weizman was talking with an American guest when Dayan arrived with his wife. Weizman saw Dayan, quickly cut his conversation short, and bolted. The sudden departure had nothing to do with politics but everything to do with family dynamics. Dayan's first wife had been Weizman's sister-in-law. After Dayan divorced her and remarried, Weizman's wife refused to be at the same functions with the one-eyed warrior.

The incident underscored how small a group the leadership elite in Israel was in 1973, a fact not lost on the guest who had been talking with Weizman when he left abruptly. That guest was Colonel Merrill A. McPeak, a U.S. Air Force Pentagon staff officer and jet pilot who had flown 258 combat missions over Vietnam at the controls of a North American F-100 Super Sabre fighter-bomber. During his time in the Pentagon, he had become a close friend of the Alon family.

With all the political and military horsepower at Dvora's house that night paying respects to her fallen husband, what happened to her and her children in the months and years to come seems almost inexplicable.

Following the memorial, Colonel McPeak returned to Washington, D.C. The dignitaries and Israeli leaders stopped calling or visiting. Dvora felt forgotten in her grief. Worse, she began to wonder if her husband had been forgotten as well.

She waited to hear from her government on the status of the investigation into her husband's death. As the weeks passed, she found plenty of time to comb back through her memories leading up to Joe's murder, and she began to remember some unusual things. The trauma and numbness she had felt in the hours after his death faded, and in their place grew an abiding desire to know *why* her husband had been killed.[3]

Dvora waited for Israeli investigators to interview her. No one ever did. She waited for the FBI to contact her again. Months passed, and she heard nothing from them either. Increasingly restless, she decided to take the initiative and sought out her friends in the military and civilian leadership in hopes of gleaning some answers. She was met with stony silence every time. The reaction among the couple's old friends was so unusual that she suspected that members of the Israeli government were trying to hide something from her.

Meanwhile, the FBI had been trying to arrange a follow-up interview. As Dvora waited for the FBI to contact her, the bureau's investigators experienced repeated red-tape delays that drew out the process for months. In the meantime, all the FBI had to go on was the discussion in the Trent Street house in the early hours of July 1, 1973, and that chat with Dvora that had yielded only one clue—her sighting of the white sedan. The FBI wanted to talk to her further and see if she had remembered anything else.

In early 1974, the Israeli government finally authorized an FBI agent to travel to the Middle East to sit down with Dvora for a detailed interview. Exactly why it took so long to secure permission has been lost to history. The Alon family believes the Israeli government stonewalled the FBI, and there is evidence that the Israelis did not want the Feds to question one of their citizens. But the time lapse may have been more a logistical delay than a deliberate one. The FBI had no direct channel to Israel in those days. Arranging for an FBI agent to enter the country would have required the help of either the State Department or the CIA. In either case, the involvement of another department would have complicated matters and required additional time to communicate back and forth.

Whatever the holdup, the FBI legal attaché's office in Rome dispatched an agent to Israel six months after the night of the murder. Years later, when I received the entire FBI case after filing a Freedom of Information Act request, I discovered that the Form 302 Interview Report that the FBI created from that meeting in Israel had been blacked out. I had not tried to run down this lead until after I left the Diplomatic Security Service (DSS) and no longer had security clearance access. As a result, I could not piece together the nature of that interview until after the Alon daughters and I made contact thirty-three years after their father's murder.

———————

I was at home one spring night in March 2007, reading through the FBI case file as my family slept, when I received an email from Rachel and Yola. An Israeli journalist named Aaron Klein put the family in touch with me after learning I was looking into the case. From this initial contact grew a relationship based on a mutual desire to find their father's killers. Later, after we exchanged further emails, they grew comfortable enough to telephone me. During that first conversation, they took turns explaining how traumatic the death of their father had been for their family. As I listened to the pain in their voices, I could not help but feel their despair. They had lived their entire lives without answers, a fact that steeled my resolve to reopen the case.

When I started asking them questions about their father and the investigation in Israel, both women teared up. They told me that their phone lines were tapped, and just calling me may have placed me in danger. This struck me as very odd. Why would anyone want to tap the phones of Joe Alon's daughters three decades after his death?

I asked them this. At first, silence greeted my question. At last, Yola began to talk.

Their mother had spent the rest of her life searching for answers and had died a few years earlier without learning anything about her husband's murder. She felt that she owed it to her husband to discover what happened, and out of loyalty to him and a fierce inner desire to know the truth, she kept going despite all the obstacles thrown in her way. Her lifelong pursuit of the truth laid the groundwork for her children to follow her when she was no longer able to continue. Dalia, the eldest daughter, refused to get involved. She had experienced enough heartbreak, so she withdrew and refused to speak of her father after she had a family of her own.

Rachel and Yola chose the opposite path. As soon as they were old enough, they joined forces with their mother. As a result, she told them everything she could remember about the night of the murder and the events prior to it. Spellbound, I listened to some of what had to have been redacted from the FBI's 302 report on the interview with Dvora Alon in 1974.

About a week before the June 30 party, Dvora began to feel as if she were being watched. At first, it was just that odd, tingly sensation people have reported when a hidden intruder has their eyes on them. But one morning, while Dvora was working in the kitchen, she glanced up to see someone staring at her through the window. In a flash, he moved away, and no trace of him was ever found. Her glimpse was so fleeting that she was unable to give a description of him, other than his gender.

Then came the phone call. The Alons had lived on Trent Street for almost three years. Their names were in the Bethesda phone book; they had made no effort to conceal themselves. One day Dvora answered the phone. In Hebrew, a man asked to talk with a person whose name she found unfamiliar. She told the caller that the individual did not live at the address and that he must have the wrong number. The caller hung up without saying another word. After the murder, Dvora remembered that call and thought it strange that someone dialing the wrong number would be able to speak her language.

A few days before July 1, 1973, someone came to the Alons' front door and rang the bell. When Dvora answered, a man wearing a Washington Gas & Light Company's uniform greeted her brusquely. He told her he was a meter reader and needed to check the gas lines in the basement. Thinking nothing of it, Dvora opened the door and let the man inside. The man disappeared into the basement for several minutes, then left the house without saying another word to her.

In fact, however, there were no gas lines in the basement. After thinking about this encounter for months after her husband was murdered, Dvora concluded that the man might have accessed the basement to tap their phone line.

While I was with the DSS, I spent considerable time studying assassinations and terrorist attacks in an effort to find ways to foil such plots before they could be carried out. This research was a major part of my job at the time, since part of the DSS's mission included protecting foreign dignitaries in the same way that the Secret Service provides security for the president of the United States. In my years with the DSS, I took part in many such operations.

Over the years, my organization began to realize that the bubble of protection we bodyguards could provide was actually quite small and could be penetrated easily. This happened in the early 1990s to the Israelis, when a lone gunman assassinated Prime Minister Yitzhak Rabin in Tel Aviv.

At the DSS, we developed a means to expand that bubble. Instead of simply posting bodyguards, we attached surveillance teams to all our security details. Their job was to scan for threats before and during the dignitary's visit. They looked for anything out of the ordinary, whether it was a person who lingered too long in one place for no apparent reason or agitated onlookers.

After analyzing assassinations and terrorist attacks, we discovered a pattern. First, the organization carrying out the attack would develop a target list. Then, once the target was selected, operatives would be sent out to conduct preoperational surveillance. They would study the target from afar, perhaps take photos and draw maps. They would next gather intelligence on the security around the target and determine the best entrance and egress routes for the attack team. Finally, once all that data was compiled, it would be used to plan the operation and brief those assigned to carry it out.

When I left the DSS and joined Strategic Forecasting, I continued working in this field for private individuals and organizations. More than once after 9/11 our efforts detected such preoperational surveillance across the country. In one case, Arab males using video cameras had conducted reconnaissance on Jewish community centers and day care facilities in multiple cities simultaneously. Cameras we had installed caught them in the act.

Having information that attackers were conducting reconnaissance missions could lead to heightened security and a change in the target's patterns. We learned that often the best time to foil a terrorist attack or assassination is not when it is under way but when it is in the preoperational surveillance stage. If you make it difficult for the scout team to get intelligence on a target, more often than not the team will abandon the mission and look for an easier hit.

That night, as I listened to two of Joe Alon's daughters tell me the things their mother had experienced before her husband's murder, it became clear to me that the Trent Street house had been the target of a preoperational surveillance mission.

First, there was the physical presence of a stranger on the property. Perhaps he was a mere voyeur or peeping Tom; I would have considered that more plausible, had the other events not taken place so close to Dvora's seeing him outside the kitchen window. The kitchen was located on the right side of the house on the opposite end to the garage. Whoever the man was, he had not just been standing in the front yard and could not be a mere passerby. He had moved off the sidewalk and stationed himself in the side yard. If he was, as I suspect, part of a preoperational surveillance team, his primary mission would have been to gather information on who was home and the physical layout of the house and neighborhood.

Second, the phone call was the next red flag for me. Back in the days before cell phones and instant communication, intelligence agencies and terrorist organizations frequently used phones to locate a target. In the espionage business, this is known as a ruse call. If a human target answered the phone, his or her location could be fixed. If the target did not pick up, that was equally useful information. It could mean that the target was not at the location where the hit would take place. "Ruse calls" were used in the 1970s by different organizations. What was discussed during the calls never mattered. The point was to pinpoint the exact location of the targeted human being.

Whoever made the call to the Trent Street house in June 1973 knew Dvora and her family spoke Hebrew as their primary language. That suggested a familiarity with who they were, or at least where they were from. Taken on its own, the phone call was unusual. Beyond that, every other theory was speculation because so many decades had passed. There was no way to get phone records and trace the call. It became another cold lead that suggested much but revealed little.

The most troubling revelation was the arrival of the Washington Gas & Light meter reader on the Alons' doorstep a few days before the murder. Musing on all these elements after I had said good night to Yola and Rachel, I decided to research Dvora's suspicion that their phone line had been bugged.

———————

In 1973, the most common way to tap a phone was not by breaking into a building or house and placing the bug inside. That was risky and unnecessary. Instead, taps were placed on the outside lines, usually at the telephone pole where the specific line branched off to the target dwelling. Someone trying to tap their phone should not have had to go to the Alons' basement.

While culling through the follow-up work the FBI conducted after the interview with Dvora, I discovered that an agent had contacted the power company to see if it had sent an employee into the Trent Street neighborhood. This detail confirmed that Dvora had related this to the FBI agent who had flown to Israel to speak with her. Why that part of the conversation had been redacted from the 302 file puzzled me, and I have never been able to explain it.

The FBI did learn that there had been a power company employee in the area that week. It could not pinpoint his location, nor could it ascertain if he visited the Alon house. In any case, he was reading meters, not knocking on doors. The meters were all outside, easily accessible from the sidewalk.

During my time in the DSS working counterterrorism cases, I came across several Dark World assassinations carried out with a simple knock on a victim's door.[4] In these cases, the assassin usually dressed as a postal carrier or employee of some known local company. When the victim opened the door, the assassin simply shot the target and fled.

Perhaps this had been the man's true intent; and when Dvora opened the door, he had to abort the mission. He would need a reason to be there if the wrong person answered the door, which would explain his quick trip to the basement and abrupt departure. It did not seem out of the realm of possibility.

Unfortunately, by the time agents began looking into the leads that Dvora provided to the FBI agent in early 1974, they had all gone cold. Had they known right after the murder in July about the three odd events, they might have been able to learn something. But six months later, the leads offered no further avenues for investigation.

After she had been interviewed by the FBI agent, Dvora grew even more determined to find out what had happened to her husband. When her efforts failed to produce results in Tel Aviv, in 1974 she booked a flight to Washington, D.C. Once back in the United States, and thinking that she could learn more in person, she went to see Ephraim Halevy, who was the senior Mossad agent at the Israeli embassy.

Halevy had joined the Israeli intelligence agency in 1961. Ultimately, he rose to become its ninth director. Later, he chaired Israel's National Security Council.

If anyone would know the status of the investigation into Joe Alon's murder, Dvora must have reasoned, it would be Halevy. But when she met with him, he immediately turned cold when she started asking pointed questions. He told her to stop digging, to return home to Israel and live her life. Leave the past in the past, he told her.

Halevy's reaction mirrored the responses Dvora had been getting in Tel Aviv. She did not give up, though. In Washington, she kept knocking on doors. One night, she received a visitor whom Dvora's daughters could not identify who also told her to go home. "You will not find the answers you seek. And if you persist, you will put your family in danger."

Her own government had threatened her simply for wanting answers about her husband's murder. For Dvora, the situation was made so much worse because the people concealing the truth were men who knew her husband, had eaten at her dinner table. Together, they had helped build Israel from a fragile, nascent state to a strong and powerful nation. Instead of seeking justice for Joseph Alon's death, they had turned their backs on the family.

Dvora left Washington and never returned to the States. She flew home to her daughters, bitter and feeling utterly alone in her quest for the truth.

CHAPTER FIVE
CONSPIRACY THEORY

1974–2005

Dvora never remarried. In the years that followed her return from Washington in 1974, she also never relented in her search to learn the truth behind her husband's death. Even though most of her well-connected friends refused to help her with her quest for answers, she did not give up. Eventually her relentlessness paid off and she was able to gain an audience with two prime ministers in hopes of finding out why Joe was killed. First she met with Yitzhak Rabin. Their discussion must have been short, as Rabin refused to answer Dvora's pointed questions and simply told her to move on with her life. Her daughters recalled that after the meeting, Dvora received an official letter from Rabin's government that sketched the barest facts surrounding the night of Joe's murder. This did her no good, as she was present that night and knew the basic facts already.

Just before she died in 2002, Dvora managed to secure one more top-level meeting. This time she sat down with Prime Minister Ariel Sharon. Dvora must have felt sure that this graying officer who had seized Mitla Pass in 1956 would provide some answers after thirty years. Joe had repeatedly risked his life to provide close air support to Sharon's paratroopers during that pivotal battle. Those bombing and strafing runs had saved Sharon's outnumbered command. Now Dvora came to collect on that half-century-old debt.

Sharon, however, proved as tight-lipped as Rabin had been. He offered Dvora nothing but the same admonishment: keep the past there; get on with your life. Once again, an official letter arrived in Dvora's mailbox following her fruitless meeting. This one, however, came with a stunning revelation: the Israeli government had never undertaken an investigation of its own into Joe's murder.

Ever since Israel had proclaimed nationhood, the Israeli response to attacks on its citizens overseas had always been a relentless pursuit of anyone even peripherally involved. In fact, the Israelis had long been known for their willingness to act beyond their borders without the assistance or approval of foreign governmental agencies in order to mete out justice. The most high-profile example of this had been the kidnapping of SS fugitive Adolf Eichmann from Argentina in 1960. Mossad agents had spirited him out of the country aboard an El Al flight so that he could be tried in Israel. Joe Alon was murdered in 1973, less than a year after the Israelis had suffered through the Munich Massacre— the killing of Israeli athletes during the 1972 summer Olympic games by the Palestinian terrorist organization Black September.[1]

After the Olympic games, the Israelis became even more ruthless in their quest for revenge. In all the time I have spent in the intelligence and counterterrorism world, I have never heard of the Israelis backing off and letting a foreign country's law enforcement agencies handle a case like Joe Alon's murder. For some reason, however, Israel had abandoned one of its national heroes.

———————

As adults, the daughters have searched for answers as to what happened with their father. They proved to be as tenacious as their mother, much to the chagrin of successive Israeli cabinets from both sides of the political spectrum. For whatever reason, the Israeli official position on the murder never changed. Aside from the barest facts, the government refused to release any information on Joe's death.

In 1994 or early 1995, Dvora paid a call on General Mordechai Gur, who had retired and returned to Israel. General Gur had been a longtime friend of Joe Alon's. But the tension that remained between Dvora and the general after the murder was an undercurrent during this encounter. When Joe's widow pressed for information, General Gur grew uncomfortable and began to behave oddly. Dvora became aggressive and asked him repeatedly what he knew about Joe's murder. Each time she asked, he professed ignorance of anything but the barest details.[2]

Frustrated, Dvora prepared to leave. As she did, General Gur suddenly said, "Let me assure you that your husband was not Mossad."[3]

Dvora had never asked if he was. In fact, that thought had not occurred to her in the twenty-some years since his death. Her husband had been a fighter-bomber pilot, not a spy. Suddenly, though, she was not so sure.

Many members of Mossad had started out in the Israel Defense Forces before transitioning into the intelligence world. It was not beyond the realm of possibility that Joe, with the end of his military career in sight, had made that leap.

Dvora was mystified by Gur's statement, uncertain whether it was meant as a reassurance or a clue. She would never get the chance to follow up with him. Not long after this meeting, General Gur committed suicide, taking many official Israeli secrets to his grave.

After his death, Rachel spoke with General Gur's widow about her father's murder. The widow remembered almost nothing about it. In the course of their conversation, Rachel was surprised to learn that Mrs. Gur believed Joe Alon had been killed during a robbery attempt. This was the first motive that had been ruled out, yet for decades she had thought that Joe's death had been a random street crime.

The Alon women pressed on. As their mother grew elderly and infirm, Rachel and Yola continued the quest for the truth. In the spring of 2003, Rachel met with Motti Hod on his deathbed. General Hod had commanded the Israeli Air Force during the Six-Day War in 1967. He had been another of Joe Alon's highly placed friends who had come up through the ranks as the IAF grew from its humble start in the 1940s into one of the world's finest air forces.

Rachel begged the seventy-seven-year-old general to share what he knew about her father's death. Either her appeal had no effect, or the general really did not know anything. Either way, Rachel came up empty-handed once again.

On June 29, 2003, the daughters met with former Mossad chief and author Ephraim Halevy in Jerusalem.[4] Thirty years after he met with their mother, he told Rachel and Yola the same thing, though he did offer two new crumbs of information. First, he mentioned that he remained in contact with Fred Beringer, one of the FBI agents assigned to the case. Second, he noted that no motive for the murder had ever been proven.

The next year, Joe's daughters arranged a meeting with Ephraim Sneh, a former Defense and Transportation minister who had served in the IDF's paratrooper brigade as its chief doctor during 1973's Yom Kippur War. After the war, he led the medical section that supported the famed Entebbe Raid in 1976. He subsequently took command of Unit 669, one of Israel's elite special forces groups.

Sneh had his own suspicions about Joe Alon's death, and he shared them willingly with Rachel and Yola. His comments were certainly interesting to say the least. He believed that their father, while working as the air attaché in Washington, stumbled across a well-placed mole in the Israeli government. Whoever this influential spy was, he or she had been providing top-grade intelligence to the United States. When Joe had discovered the mole's activities, U.S. agents had assassinated him.[5]

Sneh admitted he had no concrete evidence to back up this version of events, but he did say that he had a gut feeling the Americans had been involved in some way. He also noted that it was quite odd how Israel's military intelligence agency, Aman, did nothing to investigate the case in 1973. When a senior field-grade officer was killed, Israeli military intelligence usually was right in the middle of trying to figure out what happened.

In 1973, Major General Eli Zeira had been the director of Aman. That year he gained national infamy as one of the leaders who ignored the warning signs of an impending Arab invasion of Israel and Israeli-occupied territories. The sudden assault, known as the Yom Kippur War, came close to breaking the IDF and destroying the Jewish state. In the war's aftermath, a commission was formed to investigate the intelligence failure. The commission concluded that Zeira had been negligent in his duties, and he was forced to resign.

At the end of their visit, Rachel and Yola asked Sneh the name of the mole that their father had found. Sneh made it clear that he suspected General Moshe Dayan.

Thirteen years in his soldier's grave, there was no way for Dayan to defend himself from such a charge.[6] Nor was there any way for the daughters to confirm it. Sneh and Dayan had both been part of the same hawkish wing of the Labor Party, so at the very least his motives for suggesting that Dayan was a traitor probably were not politically motivated. Still, the meeting with Sneh opened up a whole avenue of exploration.

In Israel in 2005, Rachel and Yola met with Major General Zvi Zamir. Zamir had served in the Haganah, the Jewish underground defense organization, in the 1940s in the same unit as Moshe Dayan and Yitzhak Rabin. He had fought in the War of Independence in 1948, after which his career skyrocketed. He took over Southern Command in the 1960s before leaving the IDF to join Mossad. From 1968 until 1974, Zamir served as the director of Mossad. After the Munich Massacre in 1972, Zamir also ran the Wrath of God squads that sought to avenge the deaths of the Israeli athletes.[7]

This was a man who knew where all the bodies were buried. Rachel and Yola sat down with him and questioned him about their father. The daughters could not get any information from General Zamir. According to them, he repeatedly denied any knowledge of Colonel Alon's death, his killers, or the motive behind the murder. Some years after this meeting, I received an email from them that summed up their reaction to his alleged lack of information: "You could see it in his eyes. He was lying."

Finally, they appealed to an old family friend to share the truth. Ezer Weizman, who had bolted from Joe Alon's memorial service in 1973, seemed like their one last hope. The daughters traveled to his home in Caesarea, where they found the eighty-year-old warrior-statesman in failing health.

Weizman was not moved by their pleas for information. Once again they left empty-handed and frustrated. Weizman died a short time later, in the spring of 2005.

Appealing to their father's highly placed old friends had not worked. Going through official channels did not work either, as the daughters received little or no response from the agencies they contacted. Frustrated and angry, they changed tactics and went to the media, hoping the Israeli press would pressure the government to reveal what it was hiding. The articles and television pieces produced on Joe's death failed to move the government to release any information. In fact, they may have entrenched the forces working against the Alon family.

Rachel and Yola told me that after the media campaign, Mossad had put them both under surveillance. They suspected their phones were tapped.

In 2006, they retained a law firm and requested the FBI case file via a Freedom of Information Act (FOIA) request. If their own government would not tell them anything, perhaps the United States would. After the Israeli government tried to block this request, Rachel and Yola took legal action. The case went all the way up to the Israeli Supreme Court, which ruled in the family's favor. The FOIA request went to the Department of Justice in Washington, D.C., and some months later eight boxes, representing the entire FBI case file, arrived at Rachel's home.

The volume of material—all in English—overwhelmed the sisters. But the supreme court had given the women their first clear victory in the battle to learn what had happened to their father. None of the information in the FBI case file had ever been shared with the family. Now they painstakingly set out to read or have translated as much of the file as possible. They discovered what I had known long before: although the FBI files contained many details and plenty of redacted pages, they could not answer the two key questions: Why was Joe Alon killed? Who killed him?

Before she died, Dvora had formulated her own theory, which she had passed on to her daughters. Based on how her old friends in the Israeli government treated her, plus the fact that Joe's death was not investigated by the normally hyperresponsive Mossad and Aman, Dvora was convinced that he had been murdered because he had learned about the coming Arab invasion of Israel. Three months after Alon's murder, the Syrians, Iraqis, and Egyptians launched a full-scale surprise attack. The Yom Kippur War cost the IDF over ten thousand killed and wounded, four hundred tanks, and over a hundred modern aircraft. The war had been the closest the Arab nations had come to destroying the Jewish state, and it sent shock waves through the Middle East for years to come due to the perception that the loss of life was due to an intelligence failure on the part of the Israelis.

The war had been fought counter to established Israeli military doctrine. Since the 1960s, Israel's defense strategy relied on its intelligence agencies to provide at least forty-eight hours' warning before an Arab invasion. If detected, the Israelis would strike first, as they had during the Six-Day War.

In 1973, the Arab nations achieved complete strategic surprise. Historians have long noted the total failure of Israeli intelligence to detect the impending blows until it was too late. As a result, the war strained the IDF almost to its breaking point. At the greatest moment of the crisis, the Israelis actually prepared to use nuclear weapons against the Syrians and Egyptians. The

United States defused that potential catastrophe by initiating a full-scale air and sea resupply effort that played a key role in the IDF's ability to recover. That support triggered the Organization of Petroleum Exporting Countries' (OPEC) oil embargo, which damaged the American economy for years. Among other troubles, this caused huge gas lines for me to handle while I was pumping gas at my father's gas station.

According to the daughters, Dvora believed that her husband had discovered a conspiracy in the United States and Israel to allow the Arabs to strike first. The United States wanted to see how its latest-generation military hardware stacked up against the newest Soviet equipment that Egypt and Syria possessed. The Israelis wanted to deliver a decisive defeat to their enemies, thus securing the future of their nation for generations to come. According to Dvora's theory, Joe had discovered this and was killed by the Americans, probably with Israeli assistance, to keep him from talking.

The information that Rachel and Yola received from General Sneh—his opinion that Moshe Dayan was an American mole and that he thought Joe was assassinated by the United States to keep Dayan's double role safe—dovetailed with Dvora's theory. They believed that Dayan could have been part of a group scheming to allow the Arabs to strike first so that the Americans and Israelis could test their weapons.

The Israeli doctrine to launch a preemptive strike on its enemies if war was imminent would have been a possible reason for this group's work. U.S. secretary of state Henry Kissinger remarked later that had the Israelis launched a preemptive strike in 1973, the United States would not have given them so much as a "nail."[8] Their last source of military hardware would have dried up, and the IDF would have collapsed under the weight of the

Arab onslaught. That did not happen. Instead, the Arabs struck first, Israel looked like the victim, and the United States opened its vast armory up to the IDF.

———————

I had never considered Dvora's theory during the years I had been working on the case. But after learning what her daughters knew, I decided I had to investigate.

Because the FBI file had nothing in it to support or discredit Dvora's theory, I had to approach the case from a different angle. Instead of the murder as my starting point, I decided to begin with Joseph Alon's arrival in the United States. If I could discover why he was here and what his assignment had been, perhaps the other pieces might start to fit together. Fortunately, to initiate this new investigative avenue, Yola and Rachel gave me the first clue I needed: Colonel Merrill McPeak's presence at their father's memorial service. Why was an American air force staff officer assigned to the Pentagon sent to Israel to pay his respects at Joe's memorial service?

In seeking to answer this question, I was led from the quiet neighborhood of my youth to the skies of North Vietnam and into the heart of a Cold War secret that redrew the political map and set the stage for two future American wars.

CHAPTER SIX
ROLLING THUNDER

1950s–1970s

Joe Alon's role in Washington, D.C., and its importance to America can be traced directly back to the aerial dogfights over North Vietnam from 1966 to 1972 and one of the most painful western military secrets of the Cold War. After dominating the skies in every conflict since 1944, the United States Air Force (USAF) found itself outfought and outfoxed in the skies over Hanoi. Flying fast, maneuverable, Soviet-built MiG fighters, the tiny North Vietnamese air force delivered stinging blows to the Americans throughout the war.

There could be no worse damage to the prestige and purpose of the Cold War–era USAF. The young officers sent into battle day after day against the People's Air Force of Vietnam (PAFV) faced appalling loss rates. A fighter-bomber pilot's life expectancy was sixty-six missions. It took a hundred to complete a tour and get home.[1]

Even as they faced off against the North Vietnamese MiGs and surface-to-air missile batteries, American pilots could not help but wonder what would happen to them if war broke out in Europe someday and they faced the full might of the Soviet Air Defense Forces. In that scenario, they would not face a few scattered MiGs flown by inexperienced aviators, as they encountered over North Vietnam. They would face the best Soviet fliers in overwhelming numbers. If the USAF could not defeat the North Vietnamese MiG menace, how would its units protect western Europe if World War III erupted?

The air war in Southeast Asia had become a proving ground that pitted the latest Soviet aircraft and technology against the best the United States had to offer. It proved that the Soviets would have slaughtered the USAF in the event of a Soviet bloc offensive against the North Atlantic Treaty Organization (NATO).

During the Korean War, the USAF claimed a seven-to-one kill rate over the Communist MiG-15s it faced. Despite the fact that the USAF was heavily outnumbered and faced a very good fighter in the MiG-15, its tactics and training carried the day. Yet only a generation later, the USAF could not conquer an air force a fraction of its size over North Vietnam. Even worse, that air force kept inflicting jarring defeats on the USAF's strike aircraft.[2]

By late 1967, the days of seven-to-one kill ratios were long past. From October 1967 until President Lyndon Johnson suspended air operations over North Vietnam in 1968, the MiGs scored a five-to-one kill rate against the USAF's latest jet fighters and fighter-bombers. As the Pentagon brass viewed the disaster in Southeast Asia through the prism of a potential world war in Europe, they grew extremely worried. The Soviets were better trained and even better equipped than the PAFV and outnumbered the NATO air forces by a huge margin. A five-to-one kill rate in a European war would ensure a complete aerial defeat. Without control of the air, any general war involving NATO would end in disaster, and the free world would face total Soviet domination.

Shockingly, the USAF knew this would happen. In the spring of 1966, a series of training operations, known as Featherduster I and II, tested its F-4 and F-105 pilots in mock combat against the older but more maneuverable F-86 Sabres. The F-86s were the counterparts of the lightweight MiG-17s and MiG-21s that the North Vietnamese fielded at the time. Based on these stateside exercises, it was predicted that the MiG-21s would dominate the F-4s and F-105s with a three-to-one to four-to-one kill rate.[3]

When this prediction came true in 1967, the daily air battles over North Vietnam triggered a crisis within the U.S. military establishment. In the Pentagon, the Defense Department's Weapons System Evaluation Group undertook a series of analytical studies, called the Red Baron Reports, that examined every air-to-air engagement of the Vietnam War to date based on interviews with all the surviving American air crews, after-action debriefing notes, and other documents.[4]

The Red Baron Reports concluded that the U.S. Navy (USN) was substantially outperforming the USAF in the skies over North Vietnam. As if struggling against a third world MiG force were not humiliating enough, learning that the navy's jets and pilots were winning their chunk of the air war led to considerable interservice rancor. The reports placed the blame squarely on the USAF's lack of realistic air combat training for its fighter pilots. Postwar interviews with USAF air crews dovetailed with this conclusion; almost every flier interviewed stated he had not received the training needed to survive in the hostile skies over North Vietnam.

The reports only touched on the heart of the matter. Revamping the fighter pilots' training would not have been difficult except for a number of deeply rooted dysfunctional issues that existed in the air force of the 1960s. All had their origins in the aftermath of the Korean War as new technologies were developed and the air force decided how they should be used in battle.

———————

By the mid-1950s, the first jets capable of breaking Mach 2—twice the speed of sound—came into USAF service. Some were designed as ultra-fast interceptors that could shoot down incoming Soviet nuclear bombers before they could reach targets in the United States. Coupled with the development of guided missiles, such as the Sidewinder and Sparrow, the dogfights of World War I, World War II, and Korea were a thing of the past—or so USAF thinkers believed. Future air wars, they felt, would be fought over the horizon with radar and long-range guided missiles.

In such an environment, when even sighting an enemy plane would be a rarity, why would fighters need guns? Couldn't the weight and space be used to carry extra missiles instead? Defense Secretary Robert McNamara summed this theory up best in 1964: "In the context of modern air warfare, the idea of a fighter being equipped with a gun is as archaic as warfare with a bow and arrow."[5]

As these design and doctrine developments took place in the 1950s, the USAF changed how it trained its pilots for air combat. Part of this change was traced to the new philosophy of air warfare. Why did pilots need to practice air combat maneuvering—dogfighting—when the day of the dogfight had been eclipsed by the missile age? It seemed a waste of time. Besides, such maneuvers produced numerous accidents, costing pilots and aircraft the USAF could not afford to lose.

From 1953 until 1964, the USAF engaged in *no* active air combat missions. This time of great atrophy led directly to many of the failures evident during the Vietnam air war. As the Americans were trying to forecast what the next war would be like, however, Joe Alon and his Israeli comrades were actually fighting it, even though the IAF was much smaller than the USAF. There is no substitute for combat experience, and when lives are on the line and the fate of a nation rests with a small group of aviators, an air force does not have the option to be wrong.

With near-constant combat and an ever-present threat presented by the Egyptian and Syrian air forces, the Israelis did not have the luxury of forecasting what the next war would be like. They were too busy fighting the current one, learning its lessons, and tailoring their squadrons to meet the twin challenges of long odds and rapidly evolving technology.

The USAF leadership did not have that forge upon which to craft doctrine and training. Instead, as the 1950s passed, planning and forecasting in the United States became increasingly divorced from reality. The Israelis, in contrast, remained grounded, thanks to operational-level leaders, including Joe Alon. The knowledge and experience gained in combat shaped the Israelis' training regimens. In the process, thanks to the dedication and courage of their aviators, the Israelis forged the most effective air force of its era.

In the United States, with no imminent threat, the slide into unpreparedness continued throughout the 1950s. With the arrival of Mach 2 jets, missiles, and the first electronic avionics came the inevitable aftermath of revolutionary technology: frequent system failures. Over the decade, the USAF suffered from an exceptionally high loss rate during normal peacetime flying operations. Jets went down and pilots died every day.

With the incredible speeds and immature technology claiming lives, the USAF sought to minimize risks in training operations. Safe flying became the order of the day. Horsing fighters around in seven-G turns in mock dogfights was not only frowned on; ultimately the USAF banned it altogether. Pilots caught dogfighting could face courts-martial that could end their careers.

Joe Alon took command of the first Mach 2 Mirage III aircraft squadron in the IAF. His policies and training program ensured that his pilots would be thoroughly prepared for combat. Alon recognized that curtailing training would have weakened Israel's ability to respond to the Egyptian and Syrian threats. Thanks to Alon's stewardship of that first Mirage III unit, the IAF found the right balance between realistic training and safety. In the United States, the USAF of the 1950s and 1960s never did; its policies focused on safety and survival over realistic preparation for combat.

The effects of these errors were felt a generation later in Vietnam as the USAF's institutional knowledge of dogfighting ebbed away. Succeeding in air combat maneuvering (ACM) takes considerable practice, knowledge, and tactical savvy—all skills that are easily lost in the flying business without constant training. The diehard pilots who did not buy in to the new doctrine went underground and did their best to pass on their knowledge when they could, but the fact was that the farther removed the USAF was from its peak successes over North Korea's MiG Alley, the less capable its fighter pilots became in close-range fighting.

A perfect storm of faulty tactics, training, aircraft, and weapons design was brewing by the time the USAF met the latest-generation MiGs over Hanoi in 1966. Combat has a way of unmasking all of these deficiencies quickly, at the cost of courageous men.

The problems were legion. The Soviet-built MiG-17s and MiG-21s were small, hard to see, and elusive. U.S. planes were fast and powerful, but heavy and not nearly as maneuverable as the MiGs. The MiGs darted and danced around the American strike groups, nipping at the formations with cannon and missiles. The Soviets had not discarded guns as a weapon of air combat, and their faith in that old standby was soon justified.

Over-the-horizon battles like the ones envisioned by USAF planners a decade before simply did not exist over North Vietnam. For one thing, the rules of engagement required that USAF pilots have a visual confirmation of their targets before they launched a missile. Because of their small size, MiGs were very hard to see; pilots had to get in close to score a kill. U.S. missiles had minimum as well as maximum ranges. All too often, the USAF pilots were in a position to kill a MiG but were too close to fire a Sidewinder.

The missile technology also failed to perform as advertised. The vaunted Sparrow missile suffered a 70 percent failure rate in combat. Some exploded directly in front of the launching U.S. fighter. Some just fell off the underwing rails and never fired their rocket motors. They tumbled earthward, useless.

When they did work, the performance envelopes of the missiles were so narrow that the pilots could not score kills. Early Sidewinders could not be fired at an enemy coming head-on. To fire a Sparrow, the firing aircraft had to lock on to the target with its radar system. But USAF airborne radar systems had a hard time detecting the small MiGs when they operated low in the ground clutter. Almost 90 percent of all the Sidewinders and Sparrows fired over North Vietnam never hit their MiG targets.

In Vietnam, the USAF had brought a grenade launcher to a knife fight.

The Israelis never made this mistake, in part because initially such new technology was not available to the IAF. During the 1956 war, the Israelis scored most of their air-to-air kills with gunfire. Missiles the IAF purchased in the 1960s served as combat enhancers to the fighter units, not primary weapons. The USAF became dependent on immature technology. The Israelis did not, and even in the 1967 Six-Day War, the IAF scored plenty of kills with its cannon systems.

As the Vietnam War continued, the American pilots pleaded for guns. The McDonnell Douglas F-4E Phantom became the first latest-generation fighter-bomber to carry an internal 20mm cannon, but it did not arrive in theater until the last stages of Operation Rolling Thunder, the first air campaign over North Vietnam.[6] In November 1968, President Johnson suspended further bombing operations, and the F-4E did not get a chance to prove itself in combat in Southeast Asia.

The other primary fighter-bomber in the USAF inventory was the Republic F-105 Thunderchief, which had a cannon. But in Southeast Asia, the Thunderchiefs' main role was to bomb ground targets, and their gun-sight system focused on that role. Changing the sight from air-to-ground mode to air-to-air function required flipping five different switches located all over the cockpit, which was ridiculously complicated in combat. Pilots learned that they could not afford to take their eyes off the MiGs for so long without risking losing track of their target. "Lose sight, lose the fight" was an old fighter pilot adage that still held true. Consequently, the F-105 pilots did not bother to use the sight and simply sprayed and prayed. In this regard, the

Fokker Triplanes of World War I had a better sighting system than the F-105.

When they did use their cannon, the Thunderchief pilots discovered their gun was unreliable. One in eight trigger pulls resulted in a jammed weapon. Between its marginal ability to defend itself against MiG attacks and the deadly surface-to-air missile batteries deployed around the targets in North Vietnam, about half of all the F-105s built were shot down during the war. By the end of Rolling Thunder in 1968, the North Vietnamese MiG-21s had racked up an astonishing fifteen-to-zero kill ratio against the Thunderchief.

As the USAF lost F-105s and F-4s every day in Southeast Asia for little return, the Israelis launched the Six-Day War in June 1967. During that week, the IAF shot down 49 Arab aircraft in air combat and destroyed another 450 on the ground. Using aircraft inferior to what the USAF fielded in Vietnam, the Israelis destroyed two air forces and the bulk of Egypt's and Syria's air defense networks. The fact that these two Arab nations employed the same Soviet equipment, aircraft, missiles, and tactics as the North Vietnamese was not lost on some American observers. Somehow, the Israelis had discovered the formula necessary for victory—a formula that continued to elude the USAF.

As the losses mounted over North Vietnam, a groundswell of change surged from the bottom up within the USAF. The young Turks and squadron leaders who risked their lives every day came home with a new vision of how business needed to be conducted and began to agitate for change. A battle erupted within the air force ranks, one that the young officers won piece by piece.

In 1966, they succeeded in getting the Fighter Weapons School established in Nevada. This was the USAF version of the U.S. Navy's legendary Top Gun program. However, instead of just teaching its pilot students ACM, the Fighter Weapons School program focused on ground-attack tactics, nuclear bomb delivery, and bomber interception. It was a step in the right direction.

After President Johnson suspended the bombing campaign over North Vietnam, the USAF evaluated its performance and came up with very different answers from the Red Baron Reports. Instead of a full-scale revamping of its training program, however, the USAF brass tried to fix the problem with better technology. Unbelievably, ACM was deemphasized yet again, while the brass pinned their hopes on a new generation of improved Sidewinder and Sparrow missiles.

The navy, which had never abandoned gun or ACM training, had done far better over North Vietnam. Now, as the USAF leadership made all the wrong decisions again, the navy made all the right ones. The Top Gun program at Miramar, California, prepared a whole new generation of young fighter pilots for air combat in Southeast Asia and produced a fleet of aviators second to none.

In 1972, the USAF and USN put their paths to the test when President Richard Nixon ordered the bombing of North Vietnam again in what became known as Operation Linebacker.

The first day of the new aerial offensive, May 10, set the tone for how both services performed. The USAF's F-4s shot down three MiGs and lost two of their own. Simultaneously, the USN's Top Gun–trained pilots, supported by radar-jamming aircraft that left the North Vietnamese blind, shot down eight MiGs without losing a plane.

As the fighting continued, the USAF's performance grew worse. In June, the MiGs knocked down seven USAF strike fighters, including five in the final week of the month. In return, the air force claimed three MiGs.

Meanwhile, the USN thrashed the North Vietnamese every time they encountered them in the air. By June 14, the navy had achieved a stunning twenty-to-one kill rate. The Top Gun pilots had punished the MiG units so thoroughly that they stopped attacking incoming air strikes unless they had a clear tactical advantage, such as the element of surprise. They focused instead on beating up the overmatched USAF.

By the end of Linebacker I, MiGs had shot down eighteen USAF Phantoms. The USAF had actually performed far more poorly than it had in 1967 and 1968, leading to another round of internal angst and conflict.

Throwing technology at the problem failed. Despite the creation of the Fighter Weapons School six years earlier, the air crews assigned to Linebacker proved to be even more poorly trained and prepared than their Rolling Thunder brethren. The USAF made the situation even worse by prohibiting nonvoluntary second tours over Vietnam. By 1972, almost all air force fighter pilots had already flown a tour in Southeast Asia, which meant that only the youngest and most inexperienced crews fresh from training command ended up in theater. Scattered in their midst were a precious few old hands who volunteered to return and carry on the fight.

These young men entered the fight after being trained in a strictly supervised, structured, and safety-dominated environment. Safe flying in combat was a ticket to an early grave, and when they reached the tactical fighter wings based in Thailand, they found themselves in a brutal environment facing a complex and layered series of threats, ranging from surface-to-air missles to swift interceptors. The overemphasis on safety and structure created a recipe for failure, and once again courageous Americans paid the price for this institutional dysfunction.

Reluctantly, the USAF turned to the USN and asked for help. In August 1972, the USN obliged by sending a cadre of F-8 Crusader pilots to the USAF's 432nd Tactical Fighter Wing at Udorn, Thailand. The 432nd was the USAF's premier MiG-killing outfit, full of graduates of the Fighter Weapons School and crews considered the best in the theater.

The promising exchange degenerated into a complete disaster. The Crusader pilots engaged the USAF crews in mock air combat and simply demolished them. The USN pilots used new formations and tactics that emphasized flexibility and cooperation. The USAF relied on World War II–era formations so obsolete that they hamstrung the F-4 crews and made them easy targets.

What happened next was a result of serious cultural differences between each organization. The USN had long taught its pilots to put aside their egos during posttraining debriefings to facilitate a free flow of knowledge and learning. The only way to get better was by honestly dissecting the mistakes made so that the aviators could learn from them.

At Udorn, the USN pilots discovered that was not the way the USAF did business. Pointing out mistakes only reinforced bruised egos and inflamed passions. The USAF crews became overly defensive, and the USN pilots became appalled. When the exchange ended in September, the USN pilots wrote a scathing report and passed it up the chain of command, where it was toned down and sugarcoated for the sake of interservice sensibilities before being sent to the air force's Pacific Command (PACAF) for review.

When it reached PACAF, the senior air force brass dismissed the report entirely as interservice bias.

When the air war ended over North Vietnam in late 1972, the USAF's tactical fighter pilots returned home angry, bitter, and determined to change the state of things. The old guard that had run things so poorly tried to explain away the failure in Southeast Asia, but those in the cockpits knew that if the service did not fundamentally restructure itself, a war in Europe with the Soviets would be a slaughter. And it would not be the senior officers doing the dying.

First efforts yielded mixed results. A conference was called to discuss and debate what had happened over Vietnam. The senior general in charge of Tactical Air Command failed even to show up. Still, the young Turks pressed on. A cultural revolution was taking place, led by the aggressive combat leaders who survived their tours and wanted both a reckoning and a solution for the failures they witnessed. Too many of their friends had died for them not to pursue this. *What did we do wrong, and how do we fix it?* They wanted answers; the old guard wanted excuses. The clash was brutal, as careers were on the line.

Where could the USAF go for answers? The exchange with the USN was a disaster. Too much bad blood from years of interservice rivalries created a dysfunctional dynamic between them.

Into this vacuum stepped the Israelis. While the USAF had struggled against the MiG menace over Vietnam, the Israelis had mastered it. They possessed the credibility, combat experience, tactical solutions, and knowledge that the air force needed to foster the growing cultural revolution within its ranks. In return, the United States possessed the equipment and technology

Israel needed for its very survival. These mutual needs established a growing bond that would ultimately restructure the entire geopolitical landscape of the Middle East. At a critical time, right into the middle of that relationship, stepped Colonel Joseph Alon.

CHAPTER SEVEN
STEALING THE MiG-21

1960s–1970s

In the early 1960s, the Israeli Air Force (IAF) watched with growing alarm as the Soviet Union equipped its Arab client states with its latest-generation fighter, the MiG-21. Little was known about the new aircraft, but its capabilities were rumored to be superior to anything the Israelis possessed. Could the new MiG tip the balance of power in the Middle East? General Motti Hod worried that it just might.

With Hod's urging, Mossad set out to get a MiG-21 into Israeli hands. During the Korean War, the United States offered $1 million cash to any communist pilot who would fly a MiG-15 to an American base and defect. In 1953, a North Korean pilot did just that, although he later claimed he knew nothing about the reward. The Israelis took a page from the U.S. playbook and attempted to bribe Arab pilots into defecting.

From the outset, this covert operation ran into problems. The Soviets were so concerned about their latest and greatest fighter falling into the wrong hands that they controlled access and security to them on Arab soil, a point that rankled the Arab pilots. The Soviet Air Defense Force officers and men sent to execute this task behaved with an arrogance that reinforced Arab resentment. In Syria, Iraq, and Egypt, the pilots who staffed the new MiG-21 squadrons were handpicked for their loyalty and political reliability. To fly the MiG-21 was the greatest honor an Arab pilot could achieve.

In Egypt, Jean Thomas, a Mossad agent, managed to make contact with an Egyptian MiG-21 pilot and offered him $1 million cash to defect to Israel with his aircraft. The officer refused and reported the Mossad agent to the authorities. The agent was captured along with two accomplices, and the Egyptians hanged all three in December 1963. No doubt, this was a dangerous game. Yet, after Ezer Weizman replaced Motti Hod as the head of the IAF and continued to support Mossad's operations, the intelligence agency redoubled its efforts to get the Jewish state a MiG-21.

Mossad made two attempts to recruit Iraqi pilots after the failed operation in Egypt. Both times the Iraqis refused to defect. Then, in early 1964, an Iraqi Jew who had grown up in a Maronite Christian family in Iraq arranged for Mossad to meet a Maronite Christian MiG-21 pilot named Captain Monir Radfa. The agent sent to make the connection was an American woman who operated out of Baghdad. Although Captain Radfa was married and had children, the two of them developed a close relationship. He confided how he had been passed over for command of his MiG-21 squadron because he was a Christian. As a minority, he was so distrusted that the amount of fuel loaded aboard his MiG during training flights was closely monitored. He was not allowed to fly with long-range external tanks, even though he was the squadron's executive officer and second in command.

Radfa developed deep misgivings about the morality of Iraq's persecution of its Kurdish minority. He told his new confidante how he had been forced to fly bombing missions against Kurdish villages, missions that had become anathema to him. Once he even let slip that he admired the Israelis, for they had taken a stand despite being surrounded by Muslim nations bent on their complete destruction.

By July 1966, the Mossad agent convinced Captain Radfa to travel to Europe on a vacation getaway. There she offered him an escape from Iraq. If he could fly his MiG-21 to Israel, the Israeli government would give him $1 million and a new identity. Radfa considered it, then agreed only if his entire extended family could be pulled out of Iraq to safety as well.

Mossad went to work. A month later, on August 16, Captain Radfa took off from Rashid Air Force Base near Baghdad on a navigation training mission. He had managed to secure a long-range external fuel tank for this flight; otherwise, the MiG-21 would never have had the range to make the 486 miles to Radfa's real destination: Hatzor Air Base in Israel.

Radfa climbed to 30,000 feet and sped across Jordan on a zigzag course designed to throw off any interception attempt. He easily outflew two slower Jordanian fighters that had been launched to investigate. Once over Israeli air space, two IAF Mirage IIIs escorted him to Hatzor, where Radfa landed and officially asked for asylum.

The Israelis had just secured the Cold War brass ring. In the months that followed, their experts dissected the MiG-21's assembly, avionics, radar system, weapons, and construction techniques. After they mapped the MiG's weaknesses and vulnerable points on the ground, the IAF's top test pilots flew it to figure out its performance envelope. Eventually, it was flown in mock air combat against Israel's Mirage IIIs in order to develop tactics that could exploit the MiG's weaknesses. The plane, which the Israelis designated number 007 in homage to James Bond, served as the single greatest treasure trove of aerial intelligence the IAF had ever received. It also became a currency more valuable than gold.

This much of the story has been widely known for years, but the 007 MiG's eventual fate remained a closely guarded secret for decades. That one aircraft played a key role in the birth of a new alliance, one that reshaped the Middle East's political landscape. It also explained why Colonel Joseph Alon had been sent to the United States in 1970.

When, in June 1967, Mossad and Aman detected that Israel's neighbors were about to launch a total war against the Jewish state, the Israelis launched a preemptive attack of their own. The knowledge gained from the 007 MiG helped the IAF crush its Arab counterparts and achieve total command of the air within hours of the war's start. The one-sided Six-Day War left the Arab world humiliated and thirsting for revenge.

The decision to launch the war probably saved Israel in the short run, but the perception of Jewish aggression turned much of the world's opinion against the young nation.

In the aftermath, the French announced that they would no longer supply arms to any Middle Eastern nation. Until that time, the French had supplied the Israeli military with the bulk of its hardware. Among other things, the IAF relied on this connection for Mirage IIIs, replacement parts, engines, and weaponry. Since the Israelis were France's only clients in the region in 1967, this new policy was aimed at them as punishment for the preemptive strike that spring. The French even refused to supply weapons and aircraft the Israelis had already paid for—a fact that outraged the Israel Defense Forces (IDF) and led to a special forces operation that in 1968 stole several combat vessels out of Cherbourg Harbor that the Israelis had commissioned the French to build.

The IDF now faced the worst crisis of its short, strife-riddled history. The Soviets quickly resupplied Iraq, Syria, and Egypt with new tanks, aircraft, surface-to-air missile systems, and electronics to replace the materiel lost in the Six-Day War. The rate of resupply was so fast that despite the huge losses incurred, the Arabs soon would be far stronger than ever. By August, in fact, the Soviets had already shipped a hundred brand-new combat aircraft to their Arab clients.

With its own pipeline cut off, the Israelis were growing weaker by the day. As strategically successful as the Six-Day War had been for the IDF, it had come at a heavy price. The IAF had lost 20 percent of its aircraft and 10 percent of its pilots. The surviving fleet of Mirage IIIs had seen extensive combat and use throughout the 1960s and were worn out. The ground-attack squadrons still flew the aging Ouragans and Super Mystères from the 1950s. They too were worn out and needed to be replaced with more modern jets.

———

Now the Israelis had no source to upgrade or even maintain their aircraft. In desperation, Mossad and Aman stole the design plans for the new Mirage V and delivered them to an Israeli entrepreneur whose aviation company began work on a modified version that became known as the Kfir. The Mirage V was a ground-attack version of the Mirage III. In 1967, the French firm Dassault Aviation had already produced and received Israel's payment for fifty Mirage Vs. When the embargo took effect, those aircraft never reached the Middle East. The Kfir program was meant to fill that hole in the IAF's list of needs. But that long-term effort would take years before bearing fruit. The IAF needed new airplanes, and it needed them immediately.

To that point in history, the official U.S. diplomatic position toward Israel can be described as distantly supportive. In its desire to cultivate ties with Arab nations, the United States had largely stayed out of equipping either side with weapons. What few sales the U.S. government did allow were usually in small quantities and for defensive purposes only. That stance began to shift slightly in the mid-1960s. Shortly before the Six-Day War, the United States agreed to sell the Israelis a small number of A-4 Skyhawk attack jets, but President Johnson suspended that sale as a result of Israel's preemptive strike.

Desperate, the Israelis realized the only possible source for new equipment would be the United States. However, with the A-4 sale on hold, Israel recognized that it had to bring something more than just cash to the table to convince the Americans to do business with the IDF. The Israelis had to offer something that the Americans needed.

The 007 MiG was that offering. After the Six-Day War, the Israelis approached the U.S. Defense Intelligence Agency (DIA) and offered to lend the United States their precious MiG-21. In return, the Israelis wanted to purchase F-4 Phantom fighter-bombers.

President Johnson personally approved the deal and also released the A-4 Skyhawks for delivery to the IAF. In exchange for the MiG-21, the Americans supplied the Israelis with fifty gun-armed F-4E Phantoms. These aircraft played a pivotal role in saving Israel in the years to come; the deal itself became the first major connection between the United States and the Israeli military. It would serve as the foundation for a military alliance that became almost as close as the American relationship with Great Britain.

In early 1968, the Israelis crated up the MiG-21 and sent it to Groom Lake, Nevada—known in conspiracy circles as Area 51. There the USAF's Foreign Technology Division undertook the same rivet-by-rivet study of the MiG-21 the Israelis had conducted the year before. At last, the USAF had its hands on the weapon that was causing its fighter-bomber wings in Southeast Asia so much grief.

Dubbed the Have Donut program, the testing lasted for months, and the MiG-21 underwent a complete technical, engineering, and operation evaluation. Starting in April 1968, it was flown by USAF pilots who had graduated from the Fighter Weapons School. They tested its radar signature and compared it in mock battles against the latest USAF fighters. They also ran mock interceptions against Strategic Air Command's nuclear-capable bombers, such as the B-52, to determine whether electronic countermeasures could jam the MiG's radar and guidance systems.

Altogether, the USAF flew the MiG thirty-three times before lending the plane to the USN, whose pilots flew it another twenty-five.

In August 1968, two Syrian MiG-17F Fresco C fighters got lost on a navigation exercise and accidentally landed at an Israeli air base. This was the sort of currency that the USAF considered invaluable. Although an older design than the MiG-21, these nimble fighters were the backbone of North Vietnam's air combat capabilities and were of considerable interest to the United

States. Once again, the Israelis offered this windfall to the DIA after running their own tests.

In January 1969, the two Syrian MiG-17s reached Groom Lake, and the testing program, known as Have Drill and Have Ferry, began in earnest. The USAF and USN thoroughly evaluated the MiG-17s, then made all the data available to the Fighter Weapons School and Top Gun.

These three priceless aircraft served as the first steps toward what became a wholesale redesign of the USAF's fighter pilot training program. Although it was not implemented fully before the end of the Vietnam War, it set the stage for the awesome transformation of the late 1970s and early 1980s that transitioned the USAF into an unbeatable opponent.

Prior to the arrival of the Israeli-loaned MiGs, what air combat maneuvers were taught in the USAF usually took place between aircraft of similar capabilities. The Red Baron Reports plus experience over Vietnam showed such training to be almost useless. The MiG-17 and MiG-21 had vastly different performance capabilities, and the Americans needed to learn how best to fight against them.

Creating an aggressor squadron that mirrored Soviet tactics and aircraft was a revolutionary idea, one never attempted before. To pull it off, the USAF needed either to find more Soviet planes or to use fighters of similar performance. At the same time, the aggressor squadron would need to have a thorough understanding of how the Soviets employed their MiGs. Tactics, ground control doctrine, training methods—all of these would need to be discovered for this concept to work.

A small group of USAF officers began knocking down bureaucratic walls to get that information. They found it in widely disparate areas: the DIA, the Central Intelligence Agency, the National Security Agency, and USAF intelligence agencies all had collected useful bits and pieces. Through sheer persistence, the officers overcame each agency's tendency to guard its secret information jealously and managed to put together a clear and nearly complete version of how the Soviet Air Defense Force did business.

By 1973, the program included two MiG-21s and two MiG-17s. The United States began to scour the globe for more, along with spare parts to keep them flying. Throwing money at the problem bore good results. The U.S. government eventually bought enough MiGs from Indonesia and Egypt to form a complete squadron of latest-generation Soviet fighters. It was a monumental achievement, one that allowed the USAF to train against its most likely future enemy in a way never before possible.

But in the early 1970s, one component to this effort still was missing. While the USAF had fought MiGs over Southeast Asia for years, they had been flown by North Vietnamese pilots. For almost twenty years, no one had engaged Soviet fighter pilots in air-to-air combat. The USAF learned how they were trained and the tactics they used, and understood the aircraft they flew, but all this was theory. None of it had been put to practice with a Soviet behind the control stick. Just how good were Soviet pilots? How would they react in combat to the unexpected? Nobody knew.

Nobody except the Israelis.

CHAPTER EIGHT

THE BEAR'S BLACK EYE

1969–1970

When Joe Alon arrived in Washington, D.C., as the air attaché in the early 1970s, he came bearing the one gift the USAF needed most: information. At the height of the Cold War, those who could show the Americans how to defeat the Soviet air threat held the keys to the kingdom. Unbeknownst to most of the world, the Israelis gained that vital knowledge with firsthand battle experience against Soviet pilots and equipment during what later became known as the War of Attrition against Egypt.

In the aftermath of the Six-Day War, Egyptian president Gamal Abdel Nasser searched for a way to avenge his nation's catastrophic defeat. As the Soviets rebuilt Egypt's military power, Nasser switched strategies. Instead of open invasion, he would use the Egyptian military to bleed the Israelis dry in a long war.[1]

In March 1969, the Egyptians unleashed massive artillery bombardments on Israeli army positions on the eastern bank of the Suez Canal. Simultaneously, the Egyptian Air Force (EAF) initiated hit-and-run attacks on Israeli targets in the Sinai. The Israelis threw their worn-out Mirage III squadrons into the fray to stop these incursions. The pilots and aircraft were strained to the utmost, but the IAF scored resounding victories against the EAF. On July 8, 1969, the Syrians joined the fight. In two separate air battles, the IAF blasted nine more MiG-21s out of the sky without losing an aircraft. The testing of the 007 MiG had paved the way for these successes. The enemy's supreme fighter was a known quantity now, and the Israelis had developed the tactics to defeat it.

Despite their losses, the Egyptians continued the cross-border incursions. Their MiG pilots learned to make quick, high-speed runs on targets on the eastern bank of the Suez Canal, then dash back into Egypt before the Mirage IIIs could respond. Frustrated, Israeli general Motti Hod ordered the IAF to send Nasser a pointed message. Dubbed Operation Rimonim ("grenade" in Hebrew), the Israelis sent two Mirage IIIs over Cairo, where, instead of dropping bombs, they lit their afterburners and broke the sound barrier right over the Egyptian capital. The resulting double sonic boom blew out windows, knocked down power lines, causing blackouts, and even caused the collapse of buildings under construction. Humiliated again by the plucky Jewish air force, Nasser fired his air defense commander and ordered the trans-Suez MiG raids to continue.

Through July, the Israelis shot down so many Egyptian MiGs that the EAF stopped trying to do battle against the Mirage IIIs. At the same time, the Egyptians increased the artillery bombardments, firing more than ten thousand shells a day. Israeli losses mounted, finally forcing the IDF to launch a concerted response.

During the final week and a half in July, the full weight of the IAF was turned against Egyptian targets along the canal.

In September, the first F-4E Phantoms joined the fight. Their arrival gave the IAF its first long-range multirole strike aircraft. Able to carry eight air-to-air missiles plus seven tons of bombs three hundred miles into enemy territory, the F-4 allowed Israelis to rethink their air strategy. Instead of simply trying to intercept the marauding MiGs, the F-4s could strike at the heart of the EAF and defeat it on its own soil.

That fall, the IAF launched Operation Preeha, a systematic offensive designed to destroy the EAF. Once a week, the F-4s streaked deep into Egyptian territory to bomb Nasser's air defense network. Airfields were hit, radar sites were destroyed, and surface-to-air missile (SAM) batteries were blown to smoking ruins. Israeli pressure proved so intense that the EAF flew its bombers to neighboring Arab countries for safety. Pilot training could no longer be conducted inside Egypt, and the EAF's training program was moved to Libya and Sudan.

The siege placed Nasser in an intolerable situation. During a press conference in Cairo, he conceded that the Israelis had secured command of the air over his own nation. Shortly after that stunning admission, he flew to Moscow to personally meet with Soviet leader Leonid Brezhnev. When he arrived, the Soviet Air Defense Force's mood toward the Egyptians was one of profound disappointment. The Arabs' inability to beat the tiny Israeli air force certainly was not the fault of the Soviet-provided equipment—the same MiGs were delivering stinging blows against the USAF in Vietnam. The Soviets concluded that their Arab allies were poorly trained and did not understand the technology they had been given.

During his meetings with Brezhnev, Nasser not only demanded newer and better Soviet weapons but also called for direct Soviet intervention in the War of Attrition. Brezhnev balked at this. Sending Soviet pilots into combat in the Middle East could create a diplomatic nightmare and might even lead to war with the United States.

Nasser pressed Brezhnev, going so far as to state that if the Soviets did not intervene, he would declare the United States to be the "master of the universe" and then resign.

Reluctantly, Brezhnev agreed to send in the Soviet Air Defense Force. At the very least, this would allow the Soviets to show their Arab clients that, when used properly, the latest Soviet weapons technology could defeat any force in the world.

In February 1970, the Soviets deployed a complete air division straight from its positions around Moscow. This was one of the Soviet air force's elite units, which included handpicked pilots plus the latest SAMs capable of shooting down targets flying from between three hundred feet and over sixty thousand feet. Once this network of batteries, backed by almost a hundred MiGs, was deployed in Egypt, there would be no safe place for the IAF in the skies over the Arab nation.

———

By March 1970, the Soviets had finished setting up the new air defense system around Cairo, the Aswan Dam, Alexandria, and the EAF's major air bases. The mere presence of these batteries and MiGs forced the IAF to suspend its offensive F-4 Phantom missions over Egypt. The dynamic in the air war suddenly shifted to the Egyptians.

General Hod took exception to this. Always the hawk, he wanted to go after the Soviets and test them. The Israeli government restrained him. Throughout the spring, the Soviets appeared content to protect the strategic targets deep inside Egyptian territory, and only once did the IAF make contact with them.

This standoff changed in June, when the Soviets became more aggressive. Instead of just laying back and protecting Cairo, they shifted the air division eastward into the Suez Canal Zone and the heart of the fighting. When the Israelis detected this new threat, the government cleared General Hod to strike at the Soviet radar sites and missile batteries.

The raid turned into a disaster for the IAF. The Soviet missile crews trapped and destroyed two of the IAF's precious F-4Es. Three air crewmen died as a result. The Soviets had won the first round, and their victory encouraged them to move their air defense line even farther east into the canal zone. The IAF responded by bombing Soviet radar sites again.

———————

As the fighting escalated, the United States sought desperately to defuse the situation. The last thing President Nixon wanted to see was its new military ally in the Middle East embroiled in an unwinnable war with the Soviet Union. Quiet negotiations took place to no avail. The fighting escalated.

On July 30, a crack force of IAF pilots took off and flew toward the canal zone. Four Mirage IIIs simulated a reconnaissance flight while four more Mirages and four F-4Es waited behind them to pounce on any intercepting MiGs.

The Soviets took the bait. Twenty-four MiG-21s sped aloft from three different air bases in eastern Egypt. In minutes, they streaked into sight and engaged the fake recon flight. The other two Israeli formations piled into the fray, and soon a sprawling dogfight raged across the canal zone. The F-4E pilots nailed a pair of MiG-21s, sending them plummeting earthward in flames. Seconds later, the Mirage flight destroyed two more MiGs. The recon flight added a fifth.

Despite being outnumbered two to one, the IAF still managed to defeat the Soviets.

The situation could have quickly gotten out of hand. Fortunately, both sides accepted U.S. mediation, and a cease-fire ended the Soviet intervention. To get the Israelis to agree to the cease-fire terms, the Nixon administration offered them full access to the latest generation of U.S. military equipment and technology: aircraft, air-to-air missile systems, and even the ultra-secret electronic countermeasure pods (ECMs) the USAF had developed from hard-won combat experience over Vietnam. These vital devices could jam Soviet radar systems and protect strike aircraft from SAM attacks, something the IAF clearly needed.

The doors had been flung open, and the Israelis sent Joe Alon to the United States to share the knowledge the IAF had gained from the War of Attrition and to oversee the ultimate military shopping spree. The Israeli relationship with the United States coalesced into a partnership that helped spark a revolution in the USAF while at the same time ensuring the very survival of the Jewish nation.

In the immediate aftermath of the Soviet engagement over the canal zone, Colonel Joseph Alon took part in helping to stand up the IAF's third Phantom squadron. American aid was at last allowing for the replacement of the beloved but aged Mirage IIIs. The new squadron was to be stationed at Tel Nof Airbase, where the facilities were to be updated and remodeled to accommodate the F-4's needs.

Colonel Amos Amir, one of the IAF's legendary Mirage III pilots, had been tasked with standing up this new squadron. Working with Joe Alon, he and his men studied everything the other two squadrons had learned in order to redesign the base facilities to make loading and fueling the Phantoms as efficient and fast as possible. Joe and Colonel Amir worked closely with the base's construction unit to see that all the operational lessons already learned would be incorporated, creating the model squadron and support facility for the F-4, which would be the IAF's main fighter in the decade to come. Amir's squadron would be the template for the future expansion that was possible now, thanks to the cease-fire agreement that promised so much U.S. military aid.

Soon after finishing his tour at Tel Nof, Alon received the final assignment of his illustrious IAF career. He would travel to the United States to serve as the official air attaché at the Israeli embassy in Washington, D.C. There he would work directly under General Mordechai Gur, the military attaché. Yitzhak Rabin was the Israeli ambassador to the United States at the time.

An air attaché usually serves as a representative of his nation's air force and a liaison with his host nation's counterparts. Basically, the job is one of coordination and diplomacy, designed to foster communications between two nations' air services. The attaché is also expected to study and evaluate the host nation's air force, submitting intelligence reports back to his own government on what he has discovered. In this respect, part of the air attaché's job is to function as a spy.

When Joe Alon arrived in Washington in late 1970, he had been tasked with a special mission. He was to oversee the selection and purchase of all the U.S. aircraft, weapons, and electronics the IAF would need in the years to come. Joe Alon, who had

begun his career in the cockpit of a jet fighter swooping over
Egyptian troops fighting Ariel Sharon's paratroopers in Mitla Pass,
had been entrusted with the oversight and management of the single most important rearmament program in Israel's history.

The task would not be an easy one. The USAF's leadership
had recoiled at the idea of giving its latest weapons and aircraft to
a non-NATO nation, especially one that the Americans had not
had a deep military association with until very recently. Fearful
that such equipment could fall into the wrong hands, the USAF
protested the administration's decision.

Joe Alon stepped into the middle of this drama and used his
considerable charm to ease the situation. He made friends wherever he went and knew how to work a room. He also possessed a
profound understanding of air combat and the needs of the IAF
in the years to come. The Israelis had found the perfect officer for
this critical job.

It was in this role that he met and befriended Colonel Merrill McPeak. The USAF officer had flown F-100 Super Sabre
fighter-bombers over Vietnam in the 1960s. A dynamic, aggressive, and exceptionally intelligent young field-grade officer, Mc-
Peak came home from combat in Southeast Asia intent on
effecting change in the air force.

In 1970, he began his staff tour at the Pentagon, where he
was assigned as an air operations staff officer in the Directorate of
Plans. In this role, McPeak became one of many action officers
(AOs) who were subject matter experts on a particular region and
the issues there that affected the USAF. Initially assigned to
Southeast Asia, McPeak was lent to the Middle East desk to help
its AO review the arms package the Nixon administration had
used to induce the Israelis to agree to the summer cease-fire that
ended the War of Attrition. The AO there was not a combat avi-

ator, having spent his time in Training Command before moving to the Pentagon. McPeak was brought aboard because of his extensive experience in Tactical Air Command, combat time over Vietnam, and knowledge of the weapons systems the administration had offered the Israelis.

Right away, McPeak could see that getting the air staff to sign off on the package would be a tough sell. The Israelis wanted cluster bombs, ECMs that could jam the Soviet SAM batteries still deployed on the west bank of the Suez. The package also included Shrike antiradiation missiles designed to home in on a ground radar signature and blow the system up. More F-4 Phantoms, A-4 Skyhawks, and other aircraft were also included in the deal.

This cutting-edge equipment included some of the USAF's most closely guarded secrets. The ECM systems were particularly sensitive items.

As McPeak worked to become an expert on the proposed arms package, he also undertook a broader study of the region. He enrolled in correspondence classes on Middle East history and read voraciously on current affairs. And while he tried to keep a balanced view of the Israeli-Arab conflict, he felt himself developing great sympathy for the Israeli plight. His temporary assignment soon became a permanent transfer to the Middle East desk, where he would remain for three years.

One afternoon in early 1971, a short, dark-haired man in his forties wandered into McPeak's office. He was wearing civilian clothes and entered without a military escort. McPeak's office was in a very sensitive section of the Pentagon. Standard security procedure was to assign an officer to escort every visitor to this area so that they could be watched at all times.

Not this gentleman. He flashed a memorable grin, stuck out his hand, and introduced himself as Colonel Joe Alon, the new

Israeli air attaché. McPeak was doubly astonished that a foreign national was given free range inside the Pentagon.

During an interview in 2008, McPeak recalled with a grin that where Joe Alon was concerned, rules just did not apply. He had such personal charisma and an endearing personality that he was able to do much as he wished, even in the Pentagon.

From that first moment, a close friendship developed between the two officers. McPeak became a frequent guest at the Alon home and even celebrated Passover and other Jewish holidays with Joe's family.

———

Eventually, the arms package for the IAF was approved, setting in motion a series of exchanges that McPeak and Alon worked together to make happen. It started with the need to train a small cadre of IAF officers on the new weapons systems. In all likelihood, Joe played a significant role in selecting the pilots for that mission; McPeak arranged for the Israelis to travel to Nellis Air Force Base in Nevada and train at the Fighter Weapons School.

Five highly experienced, veteran Israeli pilots received that assignment. Joe and McPeak flew to Nevada together to greet them. It did not take long for these seven extraordinary aviators to bond in the Nevada desert. Together, they barbecued steaks, drank beer, hit the Las Vegas strip, and spent time with some of McPeak's friends who were part of the USAF's demonstration team known as the Thunderbirds. They were counterparts to the USN's Blue Angels and among the USAF's elite pilots.

The relationship between McPeak and Alon grew through 1971 and came to reflect the closeness developing between their respective nations. At one point, the Israelis asked the United

States to assist in the Kfir domestic fighter program that sprang from Mossad's acquisition of the Mirage V blueprints in 1967. McPeak flew to Israel with a team tasked with assessing the Israeli project.

McPeak made other trips to Israel over the next three years, sometimes with Joe Alon. With work done, they would travel through Israel together, and Joe would take his American friend to famous battlefields of Jewish history. On one notable excursion, they visited Masada Fortress. It was there in A.D. 73 that a force of Jewish rebels held off a Roman legion in a three-month siege. When the Romans finally constructed a ramp that could breach the fortress walls, the 960 defenders set fire to their buildings and committed mass suicide rather than be captured and enslaved by their Roman enemies.

As they walked the site of this ancient siege, Joe told McPeak how it had become a tradition for young officer cadets who were to be commissioned into the IDF's armored corps to visit this site just before their graduation. They spend the night at the redoubt, where their instructors tell them the story of the siege. The next morning, they are sworn in as new tank platoon leaders.

The arms package Joe Alon and Merrill McPeak helped manage for Israel became the lifeline that saved the Jewish nation in 1973. Without the latest-generation U.S. technology and weapons, the surprise Arab invasion during Yom Kippur would have overwhelmed the IDF. Colonels McPeak and Alon had paved the way for that conduit of military equipment and thus played an integral, if unheralded, role in Israel's ultimate salvation.

Over the years, as I learned of Alon's significance to the United States and Israel, I wondered if he had been killed because of his value to both nations. Dvora believed he had been betrayed by the very people he trusted the most. I was not so sure. In 2006, I decided to revisit the physical evidence collected in hopes of gleaning a clue that could lead to a new investigative avenue. What we discovered opened up a Pandora's box of questions and issues that two nations wanted forgotten decades ago.

CHAPTER NINE
THE FATE OF THE EVIDENCE

Late 1970s to 2007

There were two questions that had dogged me since the morning after the crime in 1973: Who had killed Joe Alon? And why was he assassinated? When, in 1981, I became a member of the Montgomery County Police Department (MCPD), I poked around in the old case to see what I could find out. There were no serious suspects and not many leads to work from. The case file gave an accurate description of the crime scene and how Joe was shot but little else.

When I joined the counterterrorism section of the Diplomatic Security Service (DSS) in the mid-1980s, I looked into the case again. I could request files from other government agencies as part of a formal investigation. The FBI file did not have much more than the old MCPD case report, but the line of investigation trended in one direction: Arab terrorism. When the FBI attempted to track the rental car and set up surveillance at the local airports, the agents were looking for men of Middle

Eastern descent. I could not find any substantial evidence to support Arab terrorism in the FBI files, however.

As the air attaché, Joe Alon became the vital link in the growing military relationship between the United States and Israel. The knowledge he and his fellow pilots shared with the USAF, the Soviet-made equipment that was "lent" to the United States by the Israelis, and the dependence that the Israel Defense Forces (IDF) developed on U.S. military hardware all made Joe's role extremely valuable to both nations. In the early 1970s, not many IAF officers had the unique mix of charisma, combat experience, connections, and political horsepower to carry out Joe's duties at the embassy. The role of diplomatic liaison, especially between nations that do not fully trust each other, is always a delicate one. In this case, with the USAF so reluctant to part with its latest technology, Joe faced a particularly difficult challenge. He defeated it with his sheer personal magnetism and the credibility he brought to the table as a combat aviator himself. In the twilight of an illustrious front-line career, he was the perfect man for the position. Replacing him after his death must have been a serious difficulty.

At first glance, given the importance of Joe's role in the United States, Dvora's conspiracy theory seemed to make little sense. According to her daughters, she went to her grave convinced that Joe had learned of the impending Arab attack and wanted to stop it. But a shadowy group of American and Israeli military leaders wanted the Arabs to initiate a war. With Israel on the receiving end of the attack, the Jewish state would seize the moral high ground it had lost during the Six-Day War. The Arabs would be the aggressors. Once they started the war, the Israelis, with America's backing, could finally destroy its enemies. Such a total victory would redraw the Middle Eastern political

THE FATE OF THE EVIDENCE

and military landscape. Soviet influence in the region would be destroyed—something the United States desired—and the safety of Israel would be secured for generations.

Dvora believed that Joe's refusal to allow his nation to face the peril of an Arab first strike prompted him to split with his Israeli superiors. With their plans, careers, and reputations in jeopardy, someone eliminated Joe and the threat he posed.

Upon further consideration, I realized that some of what Dvora believed made sense. It would explain how the killers knew Joe would be at the diplomatic party on the night of the murder, since he decided to attend only the day before. If it was an inside job, the killers would have known where he lived and at least some of his routine movements and schedule. It also would explain why the Israeli government did not investigate the case and how Dvora was treated as she sought answers in the years following her husband's death.

Nevertheless, I could find nothing in the FBI case files or in any other documents to support Dvora's conclusion. Somehow, it did not seem right. Joe was simply too valuable to both nations for either one to order his killing.

The Americans needed the information and Soviet equipment the Israelis could provide. Killing a war hero while he was on assignment in the United States would have severed the growing relationship between the countries. Why risk that pipeline? Surely, protecting a mole, even a highly placed one, would not have been worth the scandal that would have followed any revelation that the United States had Israeli blood on its hands. The fallout would have been catastrophic.

Likewise, it did not seem likely that the Israelis would kill, or allow to be killed, one of their own war heroes, no matter how desperate they were to cover something up. Joe had been a key member of the IAF since its inception. In 1973, he held a role vital to Israel's future military capabilities and had forged important connections within the U.S. defense establishment to ensure that the needs of his nation's air force would be met. What if somehow members of the IDF learned of the impending Arab attack and planned to let it happen without making preemptive strikes? And what if Joe had discovered their plans and was about to reveal them to the public? Would the IDF have gone so far as to kill him? I was not so sure about that, but the lack of a meaningful reaction by Israel to the murder of a national hero disturbed me. The treatment of Joe's family after his death, by old friends in particular, was unconscionable.

Combined, these two pieces of the puzzle strongly suggested that the Israelis were hiding something very important. I needed to look at the evidence again in light of this new theory. Perhaps with a fresh perspective and the background knowledge I had gained, something would fall into place.

In 2007, I called Ed Golian, one of the three cold case detectives at the MCPD.[1] We had been communicating on and off for a number of years, and I had found Ed and his partner Joe Mudano eager and willing to knock down doors that I could not go through anymore since leaving my job at the DSS (along with my security clearance). He was the perfect man for the job: an insider with the official credentials to navigate the maze of agencies that had information on this case. He hated red tape and bureaucratic wheel-spinning. When faced with both, he became even more determined than usual. His relentlessness usually worked wonders. Right now, I needed that energy to help run down this theory.

Later, I shared the material I had gathered on Joe's role in the United States with Ed, then explained Dvora's theory, and his interest spiked. Together, we brainstormed over how to go about proving or disproving Dvora's theory. Perhaps a fresh look at the physical evidence was in order. Since the 1970s, there had been a revolution in forensic technology. The latest methods and tests might be able to tell us something. And if anything had been retrieved that could contain a DNA sample from the killer, we might have the break we needed. But where had the evidence gone? Ed checked the MCPD records and concluded that the material had never been returned by the FBI. The last we could determine, the evidence had been at the FBI crime lab in D.C.

What did the FBI do with evidence from unsolved cases? I was not sure, but it was clear we needed to find out. But when I contacted the Baltimore field office, I ran into a brick wall of bureaucratic indifference. Nobody was interested in a three-decades-old cold case or the location of its evidence. I did manage to learn that the evidence probably still existed somewhere in some massive FBI storage facility. Bureau policy required evidence from closed cases that garnered a conviction to be destroyed after a certain number of years; not so for unsolved cases. As a result, the FBI had material squirreled away from as far back as the 1930s.

Now at least we knew that the items found at the Alon crime scene were stored in an FBI warehouse somewhere. The physical evidence included the two bullets, a few cigarette butts discovered behind the tree next to the garage, and a lightbulb that had been unscrewed from one of the front yard sockets sometime after Dalia had returned to the Trent Street house. The latter may have had some fingerprints on it. Also, the original agents on the case took soil samples, chopped down the tree the killer concealed himself behind, and pulled up bushes around the crime scene. There was also a partial palm print found on the window of Joe's car that did not match any members of the family. Getting that might prove very helpful.

I was not sure we could get DNA off the cigarette butts, but it was worth a shot. The bullets also could have been vitally important. Perhaps after all these years, the .38 caliber pistol used in the murder had resurfaced somewhere. It could have been used in another crime or ended up in law enforcement hands as a result of a post-1973 bust.

The FBI's bureaucratic reluctance and manpower restrictions almost derailed our search. We simply could not get anyone to take an interest in the Joe Alon case. The overworked agents in Baltimore had plenty of pressing issues to deal with and could not afford to devote any bandwidth to something from so long ago.

Fortunately, we cultivated a contact within the FBI who in 2007 agreed to help. Navigating the bureau's red-tape minefield, our source worked through both the Baltimore and the D.C. field offices to track down the evidence from the Alon case. This turned into a search for a paper trail. Our contact dug deep into the bureau's files. Cold-case evidence had been moved from warehouse to warehouse over the years, and at first we suspected the material had been either misfiled or lost in the shuffle. Imagine a series of storage facilities the contents of which rival an enormous library that contains the physical evidence from thousands of crime scenes. The evidence comes in all shapes and sizes—from murder weapons, like knives and guns, to, in the Alon case, a tree. Storing such varied evidence takes space, organization, and a catalog system that can ensure ready access.

Misfiled or mislabeled evidence can be sitting on a shelf somewhere, but FBI archivists would have a daunting task trying to find it. Our contact patiently worked this angle while Ed pursued others. I waited to hear from them. Gradually, they discovered a series of memos that were not in the original FBI case file.

The first clue came when our source found an internal FBI memo dated April 17, 1978. Written from FBI headquarters to the Baltimore field office, it read:

```
185-1837—4/17/78
From: Director FBI to SAC [Special Agent in
Charge] Baltimore.
In view of this case being closed by Balt. and
that no laboratory comparisons have been
conducted since June of 1977, the items
recovered at the scene and retained in the
Laboratory are being returned to Baltimore under
separate cover by registered mail.
```

At least now we knew physically where the evidence had been sent for storage in 1978. That nugget allowed our contact to narrow the search. In the meantime, I puzzled over the reference to the comparison test carried out in June 1977. What had triggered that test? Did the FBI uncover a new piece of evidence? Was a .38 caliber pistol located that some agent suspected may have been the Alon murder weapon? There was no reference to this in the FBI case file.

The next tidbit of information came from a handwritten note our source discovered on another document. The note was triggered by a request from the Cleveland field office asking the FBI lab in D.C. to run an unspecified test on a piece of evidence from the Alon case. It read:

```
On 7/7/78, SA [Special Agent] XXX Cleveland
Division, was advised that requested exam not
conducted inasmuch as evidence in this case
destroyed by Baltimore, so is this matter.
```

This had to have been some sort of mistake. We had already learned that the FBI never destroys evidence in unsolved cases. Someone in Washington must have gotten his wires crossed. More intriguing was the fact that the FBI in Ohio had some new lead in the case in the summer of 1978 and wanted to investigate it further. Again, the FBI case file does not reference any lead or request for an evidence exam in July 1978. Now we had another angle to run down. Although maddeningly vague, these two memos indicated that the FBI field offices were still discovering leads five years after the murder. Someone cared enough to be working on the case.

A few weeks after my source discovered the handwritten note, he uncovered incontrovertible proof as to what happened with the physical evidence from the Alon case. The memo, written from FBI headquarters to the Los Angeles field office on July 12, 1979, spelled out the details.

```
185-1842—7/12/79
From Director FBI to SAC LA:
Because this case has been closed by Baltimore
and all the recovered items have been destroyed,
including the single recovered bullet, no
further firearms comparisons are possible.
```

```
Therefore the submitted test bullets submitted
with reairtel [related memos] are being returned
to Los Angeles under separate cover.
```

When our contact sent me a copy of the memo via email, I read and reread it, utterly surprised. The handwritten note had been accurate after all. The FBI field office in Baltimore had destroyed the evidence in the Joe Alon case. It was an astonishing discovery. We had uncovered no prior information that the case had been closed. Yet even with closed cases, if the crime remains unsolved, the FBI never destroys physical evidence, as doing so eliminates any hope of a future conviction. Obviously, the Los Angeles field office had somehow acquired .38 caliber bullets from another crime scene that someone, for reasons lost to history, thought were somehow connected to the pistol used to kill Colonel Joseph Alon.

With the case closed and the evidence gone, there would be no way to follow up any new leads and zero chance of bringing the killer to justice, short of an actual confession. It is for this exact reason that the FBI does not normally destroy evidence.

This standard procedure was clearly not the situation with the Alon files. The evidence was destroyed, but the killers had never been brought to justice. The case had remained unsolved, and none of the details related to the fate of the investigation or the evidence had been released with the FBI files I had acquired through my Freedom of Information Act request. Until this discovery, Ed and I had thought the case remained open.

The destruction of the evidence meant that either the FBI did not want the killer found, the bureau knew the fates of those who had carried out the crime, or the leads known to the FBI at the time were exhausted. The FBI had their hands full in the 1970s with antiwar protesters, Watergate fallout, and the like.

Could the FBI have learned that the killer had died or been brought to justice elsewhere? So far, we had no evidence of either outcome. Considering that the Israelis apparently had never conducted an investigation, it seemed unlikely that the killer had been caught or killed. But that was a possibility we would need to explore further.

The possibility that the FBI might not want the killer brought to justice brought us to a dark place. In that context, the destruction of the evidence looked like a smoking gun for a conspiracy that just might prove Dvora's theory. We had to learn why the FBI might have wanted to sabotage any further probes into the murder. Could FBI agents have discovered that the CIA had carried out a hit on Joe because he had uncovered a highly placed American asset within the Israeli defense establishment? If so, that would explain why the case had been closed and the evidence destroyed.

Intrigued, Ed worked furiously to find the answers. Eventually, he uncovered a memo from FBI headquarters noting that the case had been officially closed on March 31, 1976. A supervisory special agent named T. W. Leavitt had signed the document. Leavitt also later authorized the destruction of the evidence. We did some follow-up research and discovered that Leavitt had been a Hoover-era agent, working with the bureau from 1951 to 1978. We attempted to locate him but learned he had died some years earlier. Another agent's name appeared in connection with this memo as well. We tracked him down to a nursing home, where he was incapacitated due to old age. We would get no answers from him.

———————

Eventually, we did locate one key FBI source, Stanley Orenstein. Stan had been the special agent assigned to the case on the early-morning hours of July 1, 1973. A career FBI agent, Stan had spent most of his career in the Baltimore–D.C. area, finishing his tour in the Silver Spring office. In his retirement years, he moved to the South Carolina coast. I had placed a small notice in the MCPD Alumni Association newsletter looking for anyone with information on the case, and Stan reached out to me on June 4, 2006. Having spent his career in the area, he knew and had worked with most of the MCPD cops at one point or another. He kept track of them through the newsletter.

It turned out that Stan and I had crossed paths back in the late 1970s when I was a young MCPD officer. I had been assigned to work a bank robbery case, and Stan's Resident Agency (RA) office covered my beat. He and I worked on the bank robbery together. Thirty years later, I received an email from him about the Alon investigation and learned that it had troubled him for as long as it had troubled me.

The news that the evidence in the case had been destroyed came as a complete surprise to Stan. In an email, he explained the procedures in place in the 1970s.

```
The administrative rules at the time required
the case office of origin [Baltimore Division] of
a high profile investigation to obtain FBI HQ
permission to close the case. Closing the case
meant all pending leads were covered, no further
investigation appeared necessary at the time,
and the case files should be preserved in the
event the case needed to be re-opened if new
leads are developed. I am not aware of any FBI
memo that authorized destruction of the MURDA
investigative and physical evidence files. The
```

```
case was an unsolved homicide and should have
been exempt from any file destruction program.
    I am unaware of any rule justifying
destruction of this homicide file and the
physical evidence that is a part of it.
```

MURDA was the FBI's internal code name for the investigation. Stan explained that the case had been extremely high profile and, in July 1973, had been one of the bureau's highest priorities. A foreign diplomat had never been killed before in the D.C. area, and answers were needed. The case was active for over a year, but so few leads were developed that by the summer of 1975, work on it had dwindled. Exactly what happened after that remained a mystery until Ed discovered a supplemental report in the MCPD files dated February 4, 1976.

The report was written by Detective Sergeant J. F. Lynch and referenced a conversation between himself and Special Agent Grogen of the Baltimore FBI field office that had occurred the day before. Grogen told Lynch that all pertinent leads in the MURDA investigation had been exhausted with no results. He did, however, believe that there was still the chance that the murder weapon might turn up in the future. Since the bureau still had the intact bullet found at the scene, plus the fragments pulled out of the Galaxie's front seat, ballistics comparisons could still be conducted if a .38 showed up.

That MCPD document was the only reference that could explain why the case had been closed in the summer of 1976. Stan Orenstein had no idea that the case had been closed until we contacted him. That plus the fact that the evidence had been destroyed left him quite angry and unable to believe that the case he worked on was treated in such an unusual manner.

In further discussions with Stan, we uncovered the major leads the FBI followed in the wake of the murder. Stan was a tremendous asset. While I had the entire FBI file on the case at my house, almost 90 percent of its 10,000 pages were significantly redacted. Trying to determine whom the agents considered prime suspects was like trying to piece together the Dead Sea Scrolls. There was a fragment of a sentence here, a few words there that hinted at different avenues. In some cases, just the file ID tags were left unredacted on page after page. In some cases, though, those file ID tags were clues in their own right.

In the early months of our investigation, around 2007, Stan's assistance allowed us to paint the most complete picture that we had ever had. But as we interviewed him and gathered information pertinent to Dvora's theory, we soon had a host of new avenues to investigate. Ultimately, Stan's recollections led us into the heart of a vicious undercover war that raged across the globe in the mid-1970s.[2]

CHAPTER TEN

THE SUSPECT LIST

1973

In the days following Joe Alon's death, the FBI marshaled its copious manpower in order to track down what few leads it had. The Baltimore field office formed a task force, known as the MURDA team, to spearhead the investigation and gave it the highest possible priority. Other cases were placed on the back burner so resources could be directed to Joe Alon's murder. This was the first time a foreign diplomat had been killed in D.C. in modern memory, and there was considerable political pressure to find those responsible as quickly as possible. Spurred on by this sense of urgency, those assigned to the task force devoted long hours in the months to come on their assignment.

Grunt work occupied much of their time. Initially, a team of agents fanned out through the Trent Street neighborhood to knock on doors and find out if any observant resident might have seen something unusual on the night of the murder. Though most of those interviewed didn't even hear the gunshots, the agents did pick up one telling piece of information. A few nights before the murder, Alon's neighbors who lived on the garage side of the house had heard somebody rustling around in the bushes near the tree the killer used as concealment on July 1.

This unusual clue indicated several important things: First, whoever had killed Joe probably had the house under surveillance for at least several days prior to the killing. Second, there may have been an earlier attempt to murder Joe that for some reason the killer chose to abort. Perhaps there had been other people in the area, or some other facet of the plan had failed. Either way, the neighbor's new information convinced the FBI that his death was a deliberate assassination rather than a random street crime or the act of a serial killer.

The FBI's first hint of motive came when agents reviewed the phone records from the Trent Street house. Joe had made a series of phone calls to a number in Los Angeles. When it was tracked down, Stan and his fellow agents discovered it belonged to a female prostitute. Later, the detectives discovered—probably through phone records again—that Joe had been visiting at least one woman in New York as well. A theory was quickly floated within the investigation: Could Joe have been murdered by a jilted lover? The FBI interviewed both women, who accounted for their activities in the days preceding the murder. Studying their locations and the timeline of known events, it became clear that neither woman could have carried out the killing. Neither had had the opportunity.

So, a jealous lover scenario looked unlikely after all. Operationally, Joe may have developed the contacts as "cover for status." As a professional, Joe would not have wanted to use Dvora. Frankly, it makes perfect sense to help with operational cover or to maneuver the women into contacts with Palestinian or other

Arab sources. The women would have also helped establish international "playboy" cover.

––––––––

As the investigation continued, the FBI spread out to search the major East Coast airports. In the parking lots, they looked for the white sedan or for some clue as to how the perpetrators might have escaped. That manpower-intensive chore absorbed a lot of agents and elicited no results. The car Dvora saw had simply vanished.

After talking to the neighbors, another group of agents went through a list of all of Joe Alon's known friends and associates in the United States. Joe's diary and day planner were handed over to the FBI, and there were many phone numbers from the Pentagon. This line of the investigation yielded an interesting theory. In 2006, Stan recalled that the MURDA squad had come across an old associate of Joe's who had known him since 1945. They had first met in Czechoslovakia right after the end of World War II when Joe returned from England. This friend of Joe's had survived a concentration camp only to come home to find, like most everyone else, that very few of his family members survived the Holocaust.

In the aftermath of the war, both men had chosen to leave their home country. Joe went to Israel; his friend came to the United States. When Joe was posted to the embassy in D.C., he looked his old acquaintance up, and they rekindled their friendship. During one of their conversations, Joe mentioned that in late 1972 or early 1973, a Czech Air Force colonel had made contact with him at a party. Joe had never mentioned exactly what was discussed, but it was clear that the interaction made him uncomfortable. In the following weeks, the Czech colonel made several more attempts to engage Joe in conversation. He rebuffed them each time and reported the man to the Israeli ambassador.

The Czech colonel persisted. He tracked Joe down at work and called him there. On occasion, he even phoned Joe's house on Trent Street. Each time he called, Joe refused to talk with him and continued to inform the ambassador.

Joe's old friend was convinced that the Czech colonel was trying to recruit Joe and turn him into an Eastern Bloc asset. The KGB frequently used proxies with some sort of personal connection to the targeted individual as a means to develop contact with him or her.[1] A fellow Czech aviator, a man who shared much of Joe's past, would be a textbook point man in any KGB recruiting effort aimed at Joe.

The KGB would naturally have had a lot of interest in Alon anyway. He was an Israeli hero, a man who had helped his nation defy the odds and defeat the Soviet-equipped Arab nations twice during his career. As valuable as Joe was to the USAF, he would have been even more so to the Soviets. He held the key to defeating the MiG menace, and by understanding how the older ones were defeated they would be able to improve and develop future MiGs. Had Joe turned rogue and worked with the Soviets, he could have provided that information.[2]

From an organizational perspective, the Israelis were light-years ahead of both the USAF and the Soviet air force. The IAF had learned hard lessons, applied them, and refined them in the pressure cooker of battle. As a result, by 1973 the IAF could maintain aircraft better than almost anyone else, and it could keep up an operational sortie tempo that neither superpower could hope to match. This was due largely to the innovative way the IAF refueled, rearmed, and prepped its aircraft for the next mission in such quick fashion. Having an asset within the IAF that could detail how the fighter-bomber units operated at such a peak level of performance would have been a tremendous coup for the KGB—and for the Soviet air force.

Conversely, when Joe refused to engage the Czech colonel, the KGB was likely enraged. Joe's friend told the FBI that he believed that the decision was made to eliminate him. The Soviets had a motive—revenge for the losses of their pilots during the War of Attrition. Striking back through the Dark World would have certainly been in the KGB's character. Usually, the Soviets were very cautious about potential blowback and preferred to use surrogates for such "wet" missions—a term used for assassinations associated with the KGB. During my time in the DSS, I never witnessed a case in which the KGB directly assassinated anyone in the United States. Instead, it was the intelligence agencies of their Warsaw Pact allies that frequently filled this role in the West on their behalf. So did local anti-establishment or terrorist organizations residing in the NATO democracies.

There was an element to the FBI investigation that puzzled me for years. In the wake of Joe Alon's murder, the agents assigned to the case had devoted significant time to looking into the Eldridge Cleaver faction of the Black Panthers. Cleaver had been a fixture in the Black Power movement ever since his writings had first been published from prison in the early 1960s. His book, *Soul on Ice*, became one of the leading literary expressions of the movement.[3]

After serving time for rape and assault with the intent to murder, Cleaver was released from prison in 1965. He traveled to Oakland and joined the Black Panthers, serving as the organization's minister of information. He ran for president in 1968, gaining 36,000 votes nationwide. Within the Black Panthers, he advocated an increasingly militant and violent form of social revolution. In fact, Cleaver wanted to escalate black resistance into full-scale urban guerrilla warfare. Panther-founder Huey Newton was starting to move away from violence as a means to achieve the group's goals, so the two men came into conflict with each other, eventually causing the Panthers to split.

Later in 1968, Cleaver led some of his followers in an ambush of Oakland police officers. The firefight killed one of his adherents and wounded two cops. In the aftermath, he fled to Cuba, then Algeria, where he lived in exile. While in North Africa, the communist North Vietnamese government supported him with a monthly stipend. Gradually, more exiles, criminals, and revolutionaries gathered around him. The stipend could not sustain them all, so Cleaver organized a European-wide operation, stealing cars and selling them in Africa. Cleaver did not return to the United States until 1975. But his minions had been active in his absence. In 1971, after Newton kicked him out of the Panthers, his wife established the Revolutionary Peoples Communication Network, another radical organization.

In the FBI file on the Alon case, we found a document written by the Los Angeles field office. Shortly before his death, bureau informants within the Black Panther movement reported that some of Cleaver's former colleagues had formed ten, two-man assassination teams. Who their targets were and where they would be operating was not revealed in the intelligence summary from the Los Angeles field office. That said, the FBI clearly suspected the group might have been involved in Alon's death, especially since they had the ability to carry out such operations. The Panthers were known to be radical and violent, and many members such as Cleaver had deep connections with America's Cold War Marxist enemies. They had the resources, the weapons, and a history of executing ambushes and murders. As for a motive, they may have been acting as the KGB's proxy. Further, some of Cleaver's followers were not just Marxist fellow travelers; they were pro-Palestinian as well.[4]

When I first took an interest in the Alon case, I spent considerable effort trying to confirm any involvement by the Black Panthers or their splinter groups. I came across only one tenuous connection. Back in the late 1970s, I had joined the Bethesda-Chevy Chase Rescue Squad. The rescue squad was located a few miles from Trent Street on Auburn Avenue, and the organization served as an ambulance and emergency response asset for the local area. I spent many years there at the station, waiting for the next call to send us into an unknown crisis. All that time spent with the other members of the squad fostered deep friendships that have endured throughout our lives. We would sit and talk, play pinball, and pass the time together for hours on end.

One night in 2005, I struck up a conversation with Kenny Holden about the night Joe Alon was killed. The rescue squad had responded to the scene, and both Chief Dave Dwyer and Kenny had been there. They told me that when they arrived, they found Dvora and her daughter frantically trying to staunch the bleeding from Joe's chest. As they reached him and started treatment, Joe tried to speak. Weak from blood loss, his life ebbing away, his last words fell away into stillborn whispers nobody could understand.

In the ambulance, Kenny worked to save Joe's life. The damage was too great; he was pronounced dead at the hospital without having tried to say another word.

The conversation took a curious turn at that point. Talking about that night jogged his memory, and he remembered an incident at the station that took place about a week before the murder. They had been busy with their morning routine at the station one day when a beat-up old truck rolled up Auburn Avenue and pulled into the station's parking lot. Two African American males climbed out and walked inside, looking to talk to somebody. When Kenny approached them, they asked for directions to Trent Street. Finding it from Auburn was tricky—lots of suburban streets interlaced the area, so Kenny gave them detailed instructions. They left and roared off in that battered truck, never to be seen again.[5]

The incident was unusual enough for Kenny to remember it over thirty years after the fact. There were two reasons for this. First, in 1973, Bethesda was an almost entirely white community. African Americans were just not commonly seen around town, and when they were, it was noticed. Second, the rescue squad's station was well off the most traveled streets in the area, and random visitors like the two who showed up that day were extremely rare. People simply did not walk into the station and ask for directions to any location, let alone one where a murder subsequently took place.

Any well-planned assassination requires a lot of pre-mission grunt work. The location and timing for the assassination has to be selected, decisions that are based on the target's known movements and patterns. Once the site of the operation has been chosen, reconnaissance must be carried out in order to determine the best place for the assassin to conceal himself. Entry and escape routes need to be identified and mapped. If possible, the assassin himself would want to get eyes on the area before the hit is scheduled to take place.

All of this is called preoperational surveillance. Such gathering of intelligence is vital to any assassination attempt. Even lone gunmen conduct some form of it. When an organization or agency is involved, this phase of the operation can be quite detailed as well as time and manpower intensive.

These two individuals were probably not directly involved in the assassination. If they were somehow connected to the murder, chances are they were conducting preoperational surveillance on the Trent Street house. In effect, they served as the hit team's advance party, finding the best route to the Alon residence and the best method of egress from the neighborhood.

In such scenarios, the low-level operatives probably would not have even known the true nature of their assignment. They would know only that they were to locate a specific house in a labyrinth-like neighborhood and report back what they had found. Keeping the operation compartmentalized made sense, plus snooping around Trent Street broke no laws.

Whether or not these two men were involved in the footwork for the killing has been lost to us now. There is no way to confirm it, but their unusual presence that day in 1973 was suspicious enough for my colleagues at the Bethesda-Chevy Chase Rescue Squad.

In 2007, my discussions with Stan about this angle of the case revealed that the MURDA investigators shook many trees in search of some clue of Panther involvement beyond the intelligence report on the hit teams by the Los Angeles field office. Stan explained how the FBI had fanned out across the country, interviewing Black Panther members and squeezing informants for details. All the effort revealed nothing. Nobody they talked to knew anything about the Joe Alon hit.

I contacted Eldridge Cleaver's former wife Kathleen, just to make sure I left no stone unturned. She was surprised by the FBI's characterization of a "Cleaver faction" within the Black Panthers, especially by 1973. At the time of the Alon murder, they had fled Algeria for France and were living incognito in Paris. Kathleen, who is now a professor of law at Yale and Emory University, responded with genuine surprise to my questions about the Alon case.

"If you found evidence of government cover up—well, that's what they were about, particularly the FBI during that time. I know absolutely nothing about the particular incident in 1973 . . . and even less about whatever connection the FBI was attempting to make with the blacks they thought had some connection to the 'Cleaver faction.'"[6]

In the end, the rescue squad's story became the only piece of the puzzle that even hinted at Black Panther involvement. But it was exceptionally thin, based only on the skin color of the two men stopping for directions. Despite all the energy the MURDA investigation team devoted, the Panthers proved to be another dead end.

As for the Soviets, according to Stan, the FBI could find no link between the murder and the KGB (although they had trained the Black September Organization in Moscow), nor could it find any tie with other violent leftist militant groups in the United States. Like the other suspect leads, this one led nowhere.

Given Joe Alon's military career, it seemed logical to suspect there might be an Arab connection to his murder. Alon had been a notable figure in the history of the Israeli Air Force who helped guide and lead it through its formative stages, which would have made him an inviting target for Arab terrorist groups who were always searching for ways to exact revenge. Yet, in the ten thousand heavily redacted pages of the FBI file, which both Stan and I had pored over for years, we could not find any evidence linking any Middle East group to the murder.

Though the FBI did not find any link, the press reported a connection. In the days following the crime, the *Washington Post* published a story that two Middle Eastern terrorist groups had taken credit.[7] This was not surprising. At the time, most of these organizations were still in their infancy. They were eager to make an international impression and bolster their reputations. As a result, if anything bad happened to Israel or to its interests overseas, they piped up to take the credit. An airliner could suffer a bird strike and crash; these nascent groups would claim they had organized it. I pulled out the old *Washington Post* articles from July 1973 and re-read them. The two groups that claimed to have assassinated Joe Alon were both Palestinian: Black September and the Popular Front for the Liberation of Palestine (PFLP).[8]

Whoever carried it out had left so few clues that the murder had all the hallmarks of a serious, professional hit. Just based on how cleanly the killer carried out the mission and escaped gave merit to Dvora's belief that it had been a state-sponsored assassination. If the KGB or Black Panther execution teams had nothing to do with this crime, the only remaining realistic options were the Israelis themselves, the U.S. government, an Arab nation, or a Middle East organization. The destruction of the evidence and the lack of an Israeli investigation left everyone on the suspect list.

———————

On my first day with the DSS in 1986, I found myself escorted to the bowels of the State Department building in downtown D.C.

Inside a cramped and disorderly office accessed through a thick metal door more suited to a bank vault than a government facility, I met my new boss, Steve Gleason. He was chain smoking at his desk and talking on the phone in cryptic, pseudo-code phrases that only made sense months later when I learned the language of my new job.

He looked me over and tossed a couple of thick files my way and told me that I was the new Middle Eastern terrorism expert in the office. He went on to explain that for me to understand terrorism tactics, I had to study those files. Those pages contained the prototype terror organization off which most of the groups in the 1980s were modeled. I looked down at them and saw they were marked "BSO: Black September Organization."

In the months that followed, I read and re-read those files thoroughly. Black September was a remarkably robust and shadowy group whose leadership also functioned as senior advisers to Yasser Arafat and the Palestine Liberation Organization (PLO). Formed in the wake of one of the most horrific massacres in Palestinian history, Black September served as the PLO's arm of vengeance. To operate clandestinely without attribution to the PLO and keep the PLO's actual involvement secret, Black September's leadership created a loosely organized series of cells designed to compartmentalize operations, command, and control. At its height, Black September could operate across multiple continents, had agents and sleepers in place all over the world, and could carry out shockingly violent attacks on Palestinian enemies. By the mid-1980s, no other terror group except perhaps Iran-sponsored Hezbollah could claim as many bloody successes as Black September. BSO carried out the Munich Massacre, several hijackings, and political assassinations; killed U.S. diplomats and Israeli agents; mailed letter bombs; held hostages; and attacked airport lobbies around the globe, all while operating in compart-mentalized cells or small groups.

The other group claiming responsibility for the Alon murder was the PFLP. A violent splinter group of the PLO, the PFLP was the wild-eyed stepchild of the Palestinian terror scene. With-out the cold and calculating leadership of Black September, the PFLP had been erratic and unpredictable. Its leadership had split from the PLO over a difference of methods sometime in the 1960s. The PLO continued to use violence and terror as a weapon throughout the 1970s—but used Black September as its agent for those missions, in part as a means to give the Palestini-ans a sense of hope that somebody was fighting back on their be-half. In that sense, PFLP became a competitor with Black September for the Palestinian hearts and minds.

In the meantime, Yasser Arafat, the head of the PLO, pub-licly sought to increase his role as a statesman on the international scene. To pull that off, he had to keep his distance from Black September and be very careful as to how BSO was used. As a re-sult, the targets were selected for maximum effect. The PFLP ad-vocated an openly violent approach to freeing the Palestinian people through the complete destruction of Israel. PFLP had no diplomatic presence; they were a pure agent of terror.

Later, in the 1980s, the PFLP developed international con-nections that allowed it to carry out operations in Europe against western targets. In the early 1970s, however, the organization did not yet have that capability. Striking at an Israeli official in the United States was unlikely to be in the group's scope in 1973.

Black September, on the other hand, had demonstrated it could strike at even well-defended targets on other continents by that time. It had the operational experience to carry out a clean assassination. Its dedicated followers believed in their cause and in the group's leadership and would lay their lives on the line for both. The group's avowed purpose was the destruction of Israel and the establishment of a Palestinian nation in its place. Anyone the group's leadership considered an enemy of the Palestinian people ended up in Black September's crosshairs. Its operatives were ruthless and carried out their missions with a relentlessness that more than once sent shock waves of horror throughout the world. They also specialized in high-profile targets.

On July 5, 1973, an Arabic radio broadcast from Cairo claimed that the Alon murder was in reprisal for the death of an Arab militant in Paris the week before. The victim was Mohammed Boudia, a Black September member, but I needed more details on the hit and the victim to be able to draw any conclusions.

Killing an Israeli war hero who had escaped Egyptian MiGs, missiles, and antiaircraft shells countless times would have been a tremendous coup for either Black September or the PFLP. Trouble was, while actively investigating the case in the 1970s, the FBI could find no link tying either group to the murder.

There were other problems with fingering these two terror groups as well. In 1973, neither had operated in the United States. Europe and the Middle East were the main battleground for them. There was a reason for this: until the aftermath of the Six-Day War, the United States had never been considered an enemy of the Palestinian people or of the Arab nations surrounding that Middle Eastern tinderbox. Careful American diplomacy since the Second World War had maintained balance and neutrality in the conflict surrounding Israel's establishment. Since the United States had not yet been a significant supplier of arms to the Israelis, American interests or citizens had not been deliberately targeted by either Palestinian terrorist group. Consequently, attacking an Israeli war hero inside the United States—if one of the groups did do it—not only would have represented a significant operational accomplishment but also would have marked a seminal turning point in the perception of the United States and its role in the Middle East.

From my work at the DSS in the 1980s, I developed a solid understanding of Black September's operational abilities. In 1973, it could execute attacks in Europe almost at will. To support these missions, it relied on a loose coalition of Arab intellectuals and skilled workers who had settled in Europe. When activated, they provided logistical assistance to the agents assigned to execute the operation. Usually, those agents came directly from the Middle East, thus protecting the local networks from the various European law enforcement agencies. It was a robust structure that worked effectively for years despite the best efforts of western counterterrorism units, law enforcement, and Mossad.

Black September had nothing like that network in the United States. There were no sleeper cells, no agents in place, no intellectuals living outwardly respectable lives who were capable of supporting a trans-continental assassination mission. That lack of operational ability had always bothered me and had caused me more than once to discard Black September as a viable suspect in Alon's murder. The PFLP had even less ability to execute such a mission, as they were barely even players in Europe in 1973.

In 2007, I decided to consult Stan again and get his view on this angle of the case. His firsthand knowledge of the early phases of the investigation might help fill in some of the gaps in the FBI records. He told me that everyone involved in the MURDA investigation had suspected a Middle Eastern angle. But as the files reflected, the search for clues turned up absolutely nothing to support that gut feeling so deeply shared by the agents assigned to the case. Without a doubt, it was the most frustrating element for Stan and his colleagues.

I was rapidly running out of ideas. On many occasions beginning in 2006, Ed and I brainstormed over email and the phone, searching for some avenue to continue our investigation. There were so many slender reeds, so many hints and innuendos in the case, but so few concrete leads that we both felt a growing fear that Joe Alon's murder could never be solved. Not now, not after all the years since his death. There were too many holes; with the evidence long destroyed, the chance of a conviction— should we hit the jackpot and find the killer—was remote at best.

After weeks of consideration in 2007, I formed a new plan of attack. Every terror organization has its own set of operational fingerprints. I had learned during my DSS career that they rarely changed their tactics or conducted attacks that were a radical departure from the things they had done in the past. Those fingerprints may be on the Alon case, I thought, undetected after all these years because nobody was looking for common themes or patterns. In 1973, those patterns may not have even been evident. This seemed like the one investigative approach that could benefit with history, time, and hindsight.

So far, we had been able to dig up enough information to know that it was likely Joe and his house had been under surveillance for a time period prior to the attack. We had some basic information on the tactics and techniques the killer employed. We knew that he had escaped with accomplices in a car parked nearby. Perhaps if I could go back into the history of Black September's operations during the early 1970s, I could see if there were any similarities between them and the Alon case. I would go back to the origins of the group and study the way they conducted assassinations and terrorist attacks. Just looking at the actual attack would not be enough. I would have to get into the details of their pre-mission planning, the logistical component in each case, and how those designated to carry it out were supposed to get away. A holistic approach might yield some valuable data points. Actually, whether I found any common patterns or not, the study would be very helpful. Either it would lead to the conclusion that Black September had carried out Alon's murder, or it would show no common threads, which would eliminate the group as a suspect.

After that, I would do the same with PFLP's actions.

Maybe the CIA and FBI had missed the boat back in the 1970s and did not know that either Black September or the PFLP had extended their reach to the United States. That seemed highly unlikely, but before I singled out the Israelis or my own government as potential suspects, I had to exhaust every other avenue. An intelligence failure seemed more plausible than an Agency assassination in my childhood hometown. At least, that's what I wanted to believe.

CHAPTER ELEVEN
ORIGINS OF TERROR

1967-1973

After the Israelis captured all of Jerusalem and the West Bank during the June 1967 Six-Day War, they created a zone of occupation that put hundreds of thousands of Palestinians under virtual military rule. For the proud and fiercely independent Palestinians, the situation quickly grew intolerable. Thousands fled the West Bank, preferring life in squalid and crowded refugee camps in Jordan to military occupation. It did not take long for the camps to become prime recruiting locations for the various Palestinian resistance groups, including the Palestine Liberation Organization (PLO) and the Popular Front for the Liberation of Palestine (PFLP). There were many other factions as well, all of whom were referred to in general terms as the Fedayeen, or "freedom fighters." In the months after the Six-Day War, the camps in Jordan evolved into bases for Fedayeen attacks against Israeli targets. Starting in late 1967, resistance fighters began to sneak across the border to strike at the Israel Defense Forces (IDF) or Israel's security agency, Shin

Bet, then flee back across the border to what they thought was a safe haven.

From pinprick cross-border raids, the Fedayeen grew increasingly sophisticated. In 1968, Palestinian factions conducted kidnappings, bombings, aircraft hijackings, and assassinations. Although some of these operations were well planned and executed, many Palestinian groups—not just on the West Bank but all over the Middle East and western Europe—had security vulnerabilities that were easily penetrated by the Israelis. As the violence increased through 1968 and the death toll mounted, Shin Bet and Mossad responded with singular ruthlessness. At times, they blackmailed Palestinians into penetrating the Fedayeen.

In such a scenario, Mossad or Shin Bet would identify a potential agent and study his patterns through extensive preoperational surveillance. After identifying family members, the Israelis would follow them as well, learning every detail they could. Entire dossiers were put together on the target subject's family, including photos and even films of their actions and routines. When Israeli intelligence agents would have evidence, Mossad or Shin Bet made contact with the subject. Agents would show him all the evidence of Israel's knowledge of his family, which the Palestinian would recognize was a thinly veiled threat to kill his loved ones if he did not cooperate and report on the Fedayeen's or PLO's activities.

At the same time, Shin Bet and Mossad undertook counterintelligence operations designed to foster mistrust within Fedayeen ranks. After they took suspected Palestinian terrorists into custody, during the interrogation, the Israeli officer conducting the proceedings would offhandedly mention that Israeli intelligence had turned so-and-so (naming another Palestinian). Then the detainee would be released. Invariably, the person mentioned in the interrogation room would either vanish or be found dead not long afterward.

The Israelis used this technique and others to spark internal purges within the Fedayeen. The tactic proved so effective that by early 1969, the Palestinians had become paranoid and obsessed with moles in their organizations. At least one PLO member claimed that the traitors in their ranks were generally discovered, then turned into triple agents who would feed misinformation. Palestinians probably exaggerated the number of such cases out of pride. Whether they were able to detect moles planted in the ranks of the resistance did not really matter anyway. The Israeli counterintelligence operations created discord and internal turmoil that hampered the Palestinians for years.

In the 1930s, the Germans carried out an intelligence operation designed to convince Soviet leader Joseph Stalin that the senior leadership in the Red Army could not be trusted anymore. It triggered a wholesale purge of high-ranking officers that eventually claimed three of the army's five marshals and over half of its senior colonels and generals. They were killed or imprisoned, leaving a huge vacuum in experience and ability at the highest echelons of command in Stalin's military. This had grave consequences, first in 1939–1940 during Russia's Winter War with Finland, then later in 1941 when the Germans invaded.

Through 1968–1969, the Israelis pulled off a similar coup with the Palestinian Fedayeen. The Palestinian groups leaked like sieves, and they knew it. The misinformation campaign combined with the occasional actual traitor created such an atmosphere of mistrust and paranoia that wholesale, murderous purges resulted. The Israelis watched from the West Bank as their operation wreaked havoc with their enemies.

———————

Despite the damage the Israeli counterintelligence campaign inflicted on the Palestinians, the PLO, PFLP, and other groups continued to unleash attacks on the West Bank and elsewhere within Israel. Some attacks caused material damage or notable losses of life, but others smacked of amateur hour. In one notable lapse of judgment, a group of Fedayeen recruited for a mission against Israel were brought together to train in one refugee camp. When they completed their training, the men were issued identical, crepe-soled boots. When the Palestinians tried to infiltrate this group across the border into the West Bank, the Israelis quickly tumbled to this operational security error. Security units along the frontier began watching for the boots, catching and detaining most of the mission's participants.

Other attacks were more successful. The Palestinian resistance carried out bombings in the port city of Haifa and other Israeli towns. Then in March 1968, it planted a land mine in a road across the Arava Desert. A school bus happened to be the first vehicle to pass by. When the weapon detonated, it killed two adults and wounded a number of children.

Until that point, the IDF had retaliated against Fedayeen attacks with air strikes on PLO and PFLP training camps in Jordan or Syria. Targets usually were selected based on the intelligence provided by Mossad and Shin Bet agents. The Fedayeen trained recruits in large numbers, making their camps magnets for Israeli bombs and rockets.

After the bus hit the land mine, the nature of Israel's retaliatory strikes changed. Instead of a few Israeli Air Force jets swooping down on Fedayeen bases, some fifteen thousand Israeli soldiers, supported with tanks and artillery, swept across the Jordan River and attacked the Palestinian camp known as Karameh ("dignity" in Arabic). On March 21, 1968, the IDF's assault force reached the camp and encountered fierce Fedayeen resistance. Desperate, the defending Palestinians staked everything on a last stand that bogged the Israelis down in a brutal close-quarters battle. Young boys strapped on explosive packs and charged Israeli tanks, detonating themselves as they dove under their targets. The Fedayeen fought dwelling to dwelling and sometimes room to room. Using multibuilding, walled compounds as mini-fortresses, the Palestinians sprayed thousands of rounds of machine gun and AK-47 fire on advancing Israeli troops. The battle raged for hours until the Jordanian army finally arrived and forced the Israelis back across the border.

Twenty-eight Israelis were killed; the Fedayeen lost 150 dead and another 130 captured. Since ultimately the Israelis were driven off, Karameh was seen as one of the greatest Palestinian victories of the twentieth century. Celebrations broke out all over the Middle East, and some pointed to this battle as the first step toward erasing the humiliation of the prior year's Six-Day War.

Karameh escalated the Israeli-Palestinian conflict in a number of ways. In the immediate aftermath, the news of the Fedayeen "victory" triggered a massive influx of Palestinian volunteers. Thousands flocked to join the PLO and the PFLP or any number of splinter groups. Karameh sparked a huge upsurge of support for the Palestinian fighters, which led to even more violence in the months to come. At the same time, however, the Israelis took advantage of that influx of eager recruits to plant even more agents, a fact that the already paranoid Fedayeen leadership recognized.

The Israeli incursion in Karameh placed considerable pressure on Jordan's king to rein in the Palestinians living along his border with Israel. To Hussein and his advisers, the Palestinians were guests in their country whose violent cross-border attacks caused the Israelis to attack targets within Jordan. At times, the IAF bombed Jordanian army positions in response to Palestinian attacks. Now Israel actually had sent ground troops into Jordanian sovereign territory. Tensions between the PLO and its Jordanian hosts increased.

That friction erupted into open violence in the fall of 1968. Jordanian troops ended up in a furious gun battle with Fedayeen fighters. Before the fight ended, four soldiers died along with twenty-eight Palestinians. From being a sympathetic host, the Jordanian government became openly hostile and weary of the mayhem the Palestinian presence caused in its country. The Palestinians, however, did not relent. They continued the cross-border attacks, perpetuating the cycle of violence that often killed Jordanians who were caught in the middle. Even more intolerable to Jordan was the political and social infrastructure that took root within the Palestinian camps; King Hussein's advisers viewed this as a threat to Jordan's ability to control its own territory.

In the early 1970s, when Yasser Arafat gained control of the PLO, he instituted a series of programs designed to provide comfort, stability, and infrastructure to the Palestinians living in Jordan. The PLO built medical clinics, orphanages, schools, and refugee centers as well as training camps and weapons depots. The more the PLO laid the roots for a long-term Palestinian presence in Jordan, the more openly contemptuous its members became of their Jordanian hosts, which outraged the Bedouin-dominated Jordanian army. To some in the army and the Hussein government, it appeared that the PLO was creating a Palestinian nation on Jordan's own territory.

The Israelis could not have been happier with this development. The IDF, Shin Bet, and Mossad were all stretched to the limit trying to defend Israel's borders, contend with threats from Egypt and Syria, and control the populations in the occupied regions of the Gaza Strip, the Sinai, and the West Bank. The fact that two of its enemies had turned on each other represented a tremendous short-term victory for Israel.

For the next two years, relations worsened between the Palestinians and Jordan. Ignoring King Hussein's growing exasperation, the Fedayeen continued their attacks on Israeli targets. On September 6, 1970, the PFLP carried out a series of airline hijackings that netted a Swissair McDonnell Douglas DC-8 flying out of Brussels and a TWA Boeing 707 departing from Frankfurt. PFLP terrorists on board forced the crews to fly to Dawson's Field, a remote and unused former British Royal Air Force strip in the Jordanian desert. Soon the Fedayeen surrounded the planes and their passengers. Such an international event threatened Jordan's sovereignty, a fact that outraged Hussein's advisers. Some of those closest to the king believed the Palestinians were at the point of creating a state within a state, and such brazen attacks on international targets could have a catastrophic effect on Jordan's relations with the West.

This initial attack actually targeted four aircraft. The PFLP also hijacked a Pan Am Boeing 747 and forced its crew to fly to Cairo. Once on the ground in Egypt, the passengers escaped by sliding down emergency chutes that inflated from the fuselage. The aircraft was subsequently blown up.

The fourth hijacking went amiss over the English Channel. In this case, two PFLP terrorists tried to gain control of an El Al 707, only to end up in a gunfight with one of Israel's 007 Squads, small teams of security officers who operated like U.S. sky marshals. One of the terrorists died; the other was captured. The flight returned immediately to England, although El Al regulations called for aircraft involved in hijackings to immediately return to Israel. In this case, the pilots chose to land in England out of fear for a flight steward's life. He had been caught in the gunfight and suffered five bullet wounds. He needed immediate medical care.

The decision to return to England would have a profound effect on what happened next.

The captured terrorist, Leila Khaled, was taken into custody by British officials. In response, the PFLP orchestrated another hijacking three days later on September 9. This time terrorists took over a BOAC VC-10 en route from Bahrain to London. It was flown to Dawson's Field and joined the other two airliners and their passengers. Altogether, the PFLP now held over four hundred hostages at this location inside Jordan. PFLP leaders demanded Khaled's immediate release. The British, fearing for the lives of the hostages at Dawson's Field, complied immediately. The PFLP let all but about forty of the four hundred hostages go on September 11, 1970.

The remaining forty passengers became a source of great contention. General Moshe Dayan ordered Shin Bet to round up all known relatives of the senior PFLP leadership who lived on the West Bank. Essentially, Shin Bet took them as counterhostages. All told, several hundred Palestinians were taken into custody and held during the crisis. To alert PFLP leaders that their families were now at Israel's mercy, Shin Bet allowed a small group to cross the border into Jordan to carry the news directly to their relatives.

Dayan's response was extremely effective. The passengers were released unharmed, although the PFLP did blow up all three aircraft out of spite. International media filmed and photographed the airliners burning on the runway at Dawson's Field. Soon the images were transmitted across the globe, a tremendous embarrassment for the Jordanian government. After all, this entire debacle had taken place in its country. King Hussein seemed either powerless to act against such terrorism or actively complicit with the PFLP. Neither perception was tolerable to the Jordanian government. Something had to be done; this time the Palestinians had pushed things too far.

Supported by intelligence assistance from Israel, King Hussein ordered his army to get rid of the Palestinians with a full-scale military operation against the camps along the border. On September 16, the Jordanian army attacked Palestinian command and control targets inside the nation's capital of Amman. The next day the army launched a full-scale assault into the Palestinian camps. Fighting erupted all along the border with Israel, and fierce battles raged in the streets of Palestinian-controlled towns and villages. On September 18, as Hussein's soldiers slaughtered the Fedayeen, the Syrians—long active supporters of the Palestinian cause against Israel—sent armored units across the border into Jordan to join the violence on the side of the Fedayeen. Suddenly Israel's erstwhile enemies found themselves locked in combat. Arab killed Arab as the IDF looked on from across the frontier. It was a savage, tragic display.

If the Palestinians had been able to hold off the Jordanian army, the IDF was set to launch a massive, cross-border assault to break the Fedayeen's resistance for good.

Meanwhile, as Arafat called on Iraq and Egypt for military assistance, the Syrian intervention prompted King Hussein to ask the West to come to the defense of his country. He told the United States and Britain that the Syrians had launched a massive invasion, and he needed immediate military assistance. In response, the United States put the Sixth Fleet on high alert. A division of U.S. paratroops was also made ready, ready to fly to the Middle East to support Jordan on a moment's notice. The Soviets—solid allies of Syria—did the same thing and mobilized parts of their military in preparation for war should the United States and Britain send troops into the fighting. Once again, the world was on the brink of a general Middle Eastern conflict.

On September 21, the Syrian army defeated the Jordanians at a vital crossroads. In desperation, Hussein ordered air strikes. Royal Jordanian jets inflicted such severe casualties that the Syrians withdrew and abandoned the Palestinians to their fate, a move that deescalated the situation and ensured that the superpowers would not become involved.

Now the Jordanian army sensed its opportunity had come. Years of pent-up anger and humiliation boiled over into a merciless purge that killed at least four thousand Fedayeen. Some desperate Palestinians actually crossed the border and fled into Israeli hands. Shin Bet and Mossad quickly tried to turn some of them into moles.

During the fighting, the Jordanians captured one of Arafat's most important subordinate commanders, a man named Abu Ali Iyad. He was tortured then killed. As a message to the Palestinians, his body was tied to a tank and dragged through villages, an intentional humiliation for Muslims, who, like Jews, traditionally bury their dead quickly and with dignity.

By the end of September, the fighting had dwindled. PLO and PFLP survivors escaped into Syria, where some of them settled. Others established bases in Lebanon. Without a state, without true allies, betrayed by their own, the Palestinian cause had reached its nadir.

A young Joe Alon, circa August 1940. The woman is believed to be Mrs. Davidson. Photo courtesy of the Alon family archives.

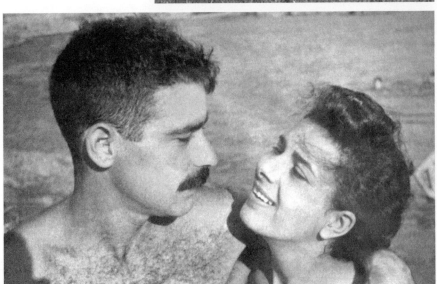

Joe and Dvora on the beach, circa 1950. Photo courtesy of the Alon family archives.

Colonel Joe Alon, circa 1955. Photo courtesy of the Alon family archives.

Joe Alon in the cockpit of the Mirage III fighter aircraft. Photo courtesy of the Alon family archives.

Pilot Joe Alon in flight suit (far left) studying a map with three other Israeli Air Force pilots.

(left to right) Moshe Dayan, Joe Alon, Yitzhak Rabin, and Mordachei "Motti" Hod, circa 1970. In looking at the pictures in the family archives, I have been amazed at the senior-level Israeli officials Joe was meeting with on a regular basis, including David Ben-Gurion, the first prime minister of Israel. Photo taken by a military photographer, with courtesy to the Israeli Air Force/Israel Defense Forces.

Colonel Joe Alon, Moshe Dayan, and Motti Hod. Photo courtesy of the Israeli Air Force/Israel Defense Forces.

Officer Ed Golian in 1975, as Ed looked patrolling the streets of Bethesda, Maryland. Photo courtesy of Ed Golian.

The crime scene on the night of the July 1973 murder. Note the bullet hole in the windshield of Joe's car. Bethesda-Chevy Chase (B-CC) Rescue Squad (Rescue 17) is in the background lighting up the crime scene. Photo courtesy of the Montgomery County Police.

Another crime scene photograph taken from the street looking toward the front of the house. The killer came from the left of the photo, after Joe pulled into the driveway on the night of the murder. The last thing you expect is to be shot or ambushed while pulling into your own driveway. The element of surprise clearly factored into the equation. Photo courtesy of the Montgomery County Police.

Crime scene photograph of the Trent Street residence lawn where the Alon family and the B-CC Rescue Squad rendered first aid to Alon. The tree in the middle of the photograph is a few feet away from the driveway and is located in the area where the shooter emerged to gun down Alon as he was getting out of his car after pulling into the driveway. The two rescue lights in the left-hand corner were used to light up the area in an effort to help the police and the FBI in the crime-scene investigation. Pillows from the house, a coat, and loose gauze bandages are also in the picture. Photo courtesy of the Montgomery County Police.

FBI Special Agent Stan Orenstein in the FBI hat and raid jacket. Photo courtesy of Stan Orenstein.

(left to right) Detective Ed Golian, Fred Burton, FBI Special Agent Stan Orenstein (retired), and Ken Holden (Bethesda-Chevy Chase Rescue Squad) in front of the Trent Street house. The picture was taken in June 2010 for a documentary on the murder for Israeli television. Photo courtesy of the author.

CHAPTER TWELVE
THE BIRTH OF
BLACK SEPTEMBER

1970

Jordan's military offensive that ousted the Palestinian resistance groups from within its borders sparked a crisis within the Palestine Liberation Organization (PLO). Yasser Arafat, who had been the head of the PLO for only a couple of years at this time, had been trying to take a more diplomatic and statesman-like approach to the quest for a Palestinian nation. After the Jordanian-led massacres, the Palestinian people wanted revenge. Young volunteers flocked to the resistance groups with a burning desire to avenge the killings in Jordan. They were not interested in diplomacy; statesmanship was lost on them. They wanted blood.

This created a problem for Arafat. The fresh wave of volunteers shunned the more moderate PLO, preferring instead to join the rival, the more violent and Marxist-oriented Popular Front for the Liberation of Palestine (PFLP), whose enemies were Jordanians and Israelis. Arafat feared that this shift meant that the

PLO would be eclipsed by the PFLP and lose its position as the "rightful" voice of the Palestinian people. He had to do something to redress this situation. In that sense, the Jordanians forced Arafat to ratchet up the violence against the enemies of the Palestinian people.

The key question for the PLO's senior leadership was how best to retaliate. Certainly, they did not want to hinder their efforts to gain international respectability and recognition. The diplomatic channels had to remain open and secure. Whatever violent retaliatory attacks the PLO ordered could not be traced back to the organization. Deniability and avoiding blowback were both crucial. If any attacks could be linked to the PLO, the fallout on the international stage could devastate the Palestinian cause. Arafat turned to his most trusted associates to conceive and execute the revenge the Palestinians so desperately wanted against the Jordanians.

For almost three years, Fatah, the political wing of the PLO, had run a special counterintelligence unit designed to track down and eliminate Israeli moles in the Fedayeen. Initially led by Faruq Qaddumi, this group, sometimes called Jihaz al Rasd or Fatah-17, included only the most trusted individuals in the movement. Qaddumi later turned over control of Fatah-17 to Abu Iyad, who ran the organization for some time until handing over it Ali Hassan Salameh. By 1970, Abu Iyad and Salameh were two of Arafat's most trusted lieutenants.

Salameh proved to be an excellent choice to run Fatah-17. A gifted thinker with a penchant for picking symbolic or dramatic locations and times for attacks on Israel, his charisma helped cement his close relationship with Arafat. His own family history also made him a natural for such a position. His father had been the leader of the Palestinian Arabs during the fighting against the

Jews in the mid- and late 1940s. During the War of Independence in 1948, he was mortally wounded in a firefight over some wells that provided water for Tel Aviv.

Salameh was not an archetypical terrorist leader.[1] He preferred nice clothing and the finer things in life and loved to mingle in the highest social circles. As a youth, he rebelled against his family heritage and his mother's attempts to force his father's mantle of leadership on him. He wanted nothing to do with the Palestinian cause. Instead, at school in Cairo, he told his classmates he was Syrian. As a young man, he earned a reputation as a playboy and a womanizer; from his mother's perspective, he was wasting his life in vice and pointlessness.

All that changed in 1967 when Salameh turned twenty-five. The Six-Day War sparked a complete change of heart. He traveled to Amman, Jordan, and volunteered to join Fatah. Arafat saw his name on a list of new recruits and sought him out, knowing how important his father had been to the Palestinian cause. Soon Salameh was introduced to Arafat's lieutenant, Abu Iyad, who ran Fatah. During a discussion in Jordan, Abu Iyad convinced Salameh to join Fatah-17.

Salameh's first assignments included tracking down and killing or neutralizing members of Fatah who had been turned by Israeli intelligence. He took part in at least twenty executions of such men, whom he considered traitors. Arafat later sent him to Cairo for special training in subversion, guerrilla warfare, and espionage. He emerged one of the most cunning and creative terrorists of his era. Yet he continued having affairs and partying, which led to his nickname, the Red Prince.

Salameh and Abu Iyad spearheaded the PLO's response to King Hussein's actions in September 1970. By using Fatah-17's most trusted members, who became the core of this new group, an international organization took shape that prioritized Arafat's need to maintain plausible deniability after any operation against the Jordanians. By then, the PLO and Fatah-17 had learned well the need to compartmentalize cells, planning, and operations. Too many moles had blown missions, leading to heavy casualties at the hands of the Israelis. In this new organization, operational security would be a top priority. Each mission would be handled by a distinct cell, members of which were kept in isolation prior to the mission. In most cases, the operatives—if they survived their assignment—would be relocated elsewhere and never used again. In a sense, this new breed of Palestinian terrorist would become like human foot soldiers. Command and control within the new organization would also be compartmentalized and informal. Abu Iyad took the lead. Ali Hassan Salameh became, in effect, the operations officer.

Unofficially, they named their new loose-knit organization Black September, as both an homage to all those who died in Jordan in 1970 and a reminder to the enemies of the Palestinian people: there would be a reckoning.

It took over twelve months of planning and building before Black September struck back at the Jordanians for the first time. Abu Iyad and Salameh selected Jordan's prime minister, Wasfi al-Tell, as their first target. He had been a solid supporter of King Hussein and a major supporter of the anti-Palestinian faction within the Jordanian government.

On the morning of November 28, 1971, a little over a year after the killings in Jordan, two Black September operatives, Ezzat Ahmad Rabah and Monzer Khalifa, stepped into the lobby of the sumptuous Cairo Sheraton Hotel. They had flown into Egypt from Beirut, tasked with assassinating al-Tell, who had gone to Cairo to attend a meeting of the Arab Defense League (ADL).

That day, after the morning meetings in the hotel, al-Tell and his wife lunched with the ADL secretary general in another location. Rabah and Khalifa sat patiently in the lobby of the hotel, eating sandwiches and drinking Coca-Cola while they waited for their target. Around them, the hotel buzzed with activity. The Sheraton was a favorite of western travelers, so the lobby was filled with American and European businessmen and diplomats.

Just before 1:30 P.M., al-Tell returned to the Sheraton and walked through the front swinging doors. Rabah spotted him as he threaded his way into the building. Cokes and sandwiches forgotten, both agents rose and approached al-Tell. Before the prime minister could react, Rabah drew a revolver and emptied all five shots into al-Tell's body. Al-Tell had reached for his own revolver, but his action was too late. Shocked onlookers watched al-Tell collapse onto the marble floor before firing a single return shot. Pandemonium broke out; people screamed and began to flee. Khalifa, however, pushed his way through the crowd until he reached al-Tell. Most of the blood spilling onto the marble came from several chest wounds inflicted by the assassin's bullets. Al-Tell did not have long to live. To the horror of the panicked crowd, Khalifa bent down and began lapping up al-Tell's blood. By the time Egyptian police reached the scene, Khalifa's face was smeared with the prime minister's blood. The horrific gesture symbolized the Palestinian bloodlust and desire for revenge that the September 1970 killings inspired.

Al-Tell's wife reached him just as he died. As she cradled her husband in her arms, his blood staining her clothes, she screamed at both assassins and cursed Palestinians and Palestine in general.[2]

Once the police arrived, not only did the Black September killers not resist, but they did not even try to escape. "I am proud! Finally I have done it. We have been after him for six months. We have taken our revenge on a traitor!" Khalifa declared after he was taken into custody. Later he added, "We wanted to have him for breakfast, but we had him for lunch instead."[3]

This first overt Black September attack was in some ways remarkably similar to the assassination of Joe Alon. Clearly, Black September had done its homework on the prime minister. It knew his schedule; it knew the hotel he was staying at in Cairo. If a countersurveillance element had been assigned to al-Tell's security detail, it would have picked up on Khalifa and Rabah spending all morning nibbling sandwiches and watching the door. The purpose of a countersurveillance team is to study a crowd or an area and look for people out of place or who are doing something unusual. In this case, the two assassins had pretended to eat for hours. A countersurveillance team would have noticed that the two were obviously watching the front entrance, a significant warning sign. Without a countersurveillance team in place, however, Prime Minister al-Tell had only two lines of defense: his bodyguards and his own revolver.

The fact that Black September knew where the prime minister was staying and his schedule meant two things. First, the organization had conducted extensive preoperational surveillance on the prime minister. Khalifa's comment that it took six months to kill him is probably not an exaggeration. They watched him during that time and garnered enough intelligence to finally carry out the mission.

Second, the assassination team flew in on a moment's notice from Beirut. They had been standing by, not participating in the preoperational surveillance. This meant either that Black September had another team of watchers on the ground in Cairo to follow al-Tell or that the Palestinians worked closely with a like-minded group already active in Egypt.

As with the assassination of al-Tell, a five-shot revolver emptied into Joe Alon at close range after a high level of preoperational surveillance. A sophisticated group was involved in both hits, there was no denying that. The FBI and Montgomery County Police Department investigations, Dvora's revelations in Israel several months after the fact, and the tidbit I had picked up from the rescue squad all suggested that a very robust preoperational surveillance and reconnaissance mission had been conducted before the actual assassination.

On December 15, 1971, three weeks after Wasfi al-Tell was murdered in the crowded Sheraton lobby, the Jordanian ambassador to the United Kingdom left his house in Kensington one morning and climbed into his waiting car. His driver pulled out onto the city streets as the ambassador relaxed in back. As they approached the intersection of Duchess of Bedford Walk and Campden Hill Road, the driver saw a man standing in the traffic island. Suddenly the man drew from his coat a World War II–era Sten submachine gun. Before either driver or ambassador could react, the gunman unleashed a fusillade of bullets on the car. Windows were shot out, the hood and doors pockmarked with holes. The ambassador took a round in the right hand while the driver lost control and crashed into a wall. The gunman emptied his magazine and fled to a waiting vehicle. After he jumped inside, it raced off and disappeared into the maze of London streets.

Both the driver and the ambassador survived. A short time later, Black September claimed the operation as its own. The Jordanian ambassador to the United Kingdom was a close friend of King Hussein's. He had been an adviser to the throne and had advocated driving the Palestinians out of Jordan. As a result, he was the number-three man on Black September's assassination list after the king himself and the prime minister.

At first glance, this attack does not seem anything like Joe Alon's murder. The target was shot at while in a moving vehicle by a waiting gunman armed with a submachine gun, not a revolver. But in reality, there were a number of similarities. Once again Black September had been thorough with its preoperational surveillance. Its intelligence gathering had discovered the ambassador's most traveled routes, his routine, and his schedule. As a result, the assassination team knew exactly where to wait for their quarry. As with the al-Tell and Alon murders, a lot of legwork had gone into the operation.

The attempt on the ambassador's life had a new component not seen in the first attack. When al-Tell went down, neither assassin tried to escape. The police easily swept them up. In London, that changed. The gunman was never caught or even identified, because he escaped thanks to at least one confederate behind the wheel of a nearby getaway car. This was very similar to how Alon's killer got away.

I wondered how Black September had learned so much about the ambassador prior to the mission. Did it have agents in place? Did it use a network of surrogates for logistical and surveillance support? Or in the year after the Jordanian attack on the Palestinians, did Black September construct a network of operatives in both Egypt and the United Kingdom and throughout western Europe?

Black September most certainly did construct such a network. In fact, through the early 1970s, its agents and operatives—all members of Fatah or the PLO—established bases of operations in Paris, Rome, the United Kingdom, and Germany.[4] With those cells in place, Black September was set to stage its most ambitious attacks yet. In doing so, its international reach stunned the world.

CHAPTER THIRTEEN

THE SHADOW WAR BEGINS

1972–1973

Although King Hussein's government was Black September's original target, its main enemy remained Israel. After the initial strikes against Jordanian targets, Black September adjusted its aim, putting Israelis right in the crosshairs. In doing so, Abu Iyad and Ali Hassan Salameh set the stage for a vicious secret war that would rage across the globe for months. In what was later called the Shadow War, both sides took casualties: well-known Black September leaders and Mossad agents died in attacks that stretched from Paris to Bangkok. As I revisited this dark period in Middle East history in 2006, I began to suspect that perhaps Joe Alon had been swept into the fighting and paid the ultimate price.

The origins of the Shadow War can be traced to a 1972 letter that the Palestine Liberation Organization wrote to the International Olympic Committee requesting that a team of Palestinian athletes be allowed to compete at the summer games to be held in Munich that September. The committee did not even reply to the letter, which Yasser Arafat and his lieutenants considered a grave insult. While discussing the matter at a café, Salameh and Abu Iyad came up with a plan to exact revenge by attacking the Israeli Olympic team during the games. With the international spotlight on Munich, this could be a devastating blow to Israel while showing the world Black September's power and reach.

Salameh planned the attack with cunning and exacting operational security. Fifty young Palestinian volunteers were culled from the refugee camps and put through a rigorous training program. At the end, six were chosen for the mission. None had any idea what that mission was, only that it was significant.

In the meantime, Salameh designated Muhammad Massalha as the commander of the assault team. A natural choice for the mission, well educated and fluent in German, Massalha was a Palestinian émigré who had studied architecture in Europe and actually worked on the construction of the Olympic Village in Munich, where the Olympic athletes lived during the games. He already knew the layout. To get a closer look at where the Israeli team would be housed, he returned to Munich and took a job in the village's cafeteria. That gave him the freedom to roam around, make notes, and conduct thorough preoperational surveillance. Thanks to his efforts, Black September gained a complete picture of the target area, including the interior layout of the dormitory that would house the Israeli athletes. Such intelligence is absolutely essential to the success of any attack.

A twenty-five-year-old Palestinian student, Yusuf Nazzal, served as Massalha's second in command for the operation. A cagey, cerebral guerrilla fighter and terrorist, he brought discipline and savvy to the effort. Together, he and Massalha were a formidable pair.

At the end of August 1972, an Arab couple from Morocco flew into Cologne, bringing with them five suitcases. As they tried to clear customs, a German official asked to look inside one of their bags. The couple protested but eventually opened the bag. The women's undergarments it contained spilled out in a tangle. Embarrassed, the customs official waved the couple through.

If he had checked one of the other bags, he would have discovered eight AK-47 assault rifles and magazines of ammunition. The couple took the weapons to Munich and left them in a locker at the train station. Before leaving the country, they passed the locker key to a Black September agent named Fakhri al Umari, who then gave it to Massalha.

Salameh had compartmentalized everything so well that neither the Arab couple nor Umari had any knowledge of the operation or its target. All three cleared out of Europe on the eve of the assault, which Salameh had code-named Ikrit and Birim, the names of two Christian villages near the Israeli border with Lebanon. Abu Iyad chose the code name as a symbol of the Palestinian desire to return to a homeland that had been torn away from the Palestinians.[1]

All of these preoperational components looked strikingly similar to what took place in advance of Joe Alon's assassination. In both cases, the surveillance and intelligence-gathering operations were thorough. If Black September had orchestrated the killing of Joe Alon, the lack of evidence, the lack of suspects, and the lack of rumors picked up by the FBI could be explained by Salameh's method of compartmentalizing operations. Security would have been very tight. In Joe's case, it was so good that it defied the best efforts of the world's leading investigative agency for years.

———————

In early September, the six other cell members culled from the refugee camps arrived in Germany and were sequestered in separate safe houses in Munich. At the last possible moment, they were finally briefed on their mission. Massalha was appointed commander of the mission.

At four-thirty on the morning of September 5, 1972, eight terrorists arrived at the Olympic Village dressed as athletes in track suits. Carrying AK-47s in large tote bags, they climbed over the perimeter fence. This move attracted the attention of the German security guards, but they did nothing, assuming that the men were athletes sneaking back from an unauthorized party in town.

The terrorists moved swiftly to the Israeli dormitory. On the front steps, they donned ski masks and passed around the AK-47s. Then they slipped into the building and sped up the stairwell to the third floor. Moving into the hallway, they knocked on the first door they reached. The Israeli wrestling coach woke up to the knocking and cracked the door. As soon as he saw the terrorists, he tried to bar the way while shouting a warning to his athletes to run for it.

The Palestinians opened fire through the door, killing the coach. One athlete was able to dive through a window and escape, but the others did not have time to react. In the ensuing chaos, Joe Romano, Israel's weight-lifting champion, was cut down by AK-47 fire. The other athletes in the area had no choice but to surrender. Altogether, Massalha's men took nine Israelis hostage. Once the Palestinians gained positive control of their captives, they gathered them in one room and bound their hands. Then Massalha tossed a two-page list of demands down to the courtyard below. It included a short declaration signed by Black September and the names of two hundred Palestinians and Arabs being held in Israeli jails whom the terrorists wanted released.

Within minutes of the attack, the German authorities surrounded the dormitory and began negotiations with Massalha. In Israel, Prime Minister Golda Meir was briefed on the crisis. At first she refused to negotiate with Black September. She favored a rescue effort, something that the West German security forces said they could attempt. Unfortunately, the local forces did not have the experience, knowledge, training, or skill to conduct such a delicate operation, and what followed was a series of errors that led to carnage.

German negotiations with the terrorists throughout the morning resulted in no concessions. In the early afternoon, the Israeli government offered the terrorists a secret deal: If the athletes were released and replaced with nine West German substitutes who would then be flown with the terrorists to an Arab nation, the Israelis would release fifty prisoners from the list a few months later. They would do so quietly to avoid any press attention.

Massalha attempted to contact his Black September superior, but a series of problems with long-distance telephone communication prevented him from getting approval to take the deal. Finally, late that afternoon, he demanded an airplane that would fly his men and the hostages to Cairo. The Germans agreed, thinking this would give their security forces the chance to effect a rescue.

After dark, the terrorists and their hostages rode in buses to two waiting helicopters. As the choppers flew to the airport, the West Germans placed a Lufthansa airliner on the flight line. Although there was no crew and the plane was not flight ready, the Germans figured they could use the plane as bait to draw the terrorists out. From there, five sharpshooters stationed around the airport could engage the eight terrorists.

The five German marksmen were equipped with slow-firing bolt-action rifles. When the helicopters landed, Massalha and Nazzal debarked to examine the nearby jet. Once aboard, they quickly realized the plane was not ready for flight. The jig was up. When the terrorists reached the tarmac again, German sharpshooters opened fire. Instead of shooting the terrorists still in the helicopters with their weapons trained on the Israeli athletes, all five Germans took aim at Massalha and Nazzal. The first volley killed Massalha and wounded Nazzal, who crumpled to the ground. The other terrorists reacted immediately. They flipped their AKs to full auto and slaughtered the Israeli athletes. Then some of the terrorists began shooting at the Germans, killing one police officer. The Germans tossed a grenade into one of the helicopters, which exploded and began to burn.

For several critical moments, an unequal gun battle raged between the slow-firing German sharpshooters and the assault rifle–equipped terrorists. Gunfire stitched the remaining helicopter, touching off its fuel tank. As both choppers belched flames into the Munich night, armored cars full of German police sped to the scene. The reinforcements turned the tide, and four of the remaining six terrorists died in a desperate last stand.

The three surviving terrorists were imprisoned in Germany.

The Olympic Games had been turned into an international tragedy. West Germany, which had been trying to use the event to reintroduce the country to the international community and erase the stain of the 1936 Nazi-sponsored Olympics, had been disgraced. Once again, Jews had died in Germany, a particularly painful reality for Israel.[2]

Altogether, eleven Israelis, a German police officer, and five terrorists died. The world reeled from the attack, which was covered by the international press in great detail. In Arab countries, the terrorists were celebrated as heroes. Israel went into a period of mourning even as its air force responded with a series of attacks on Fatah training bases in southern Lebanon.

Salameh, who had been in East Berlin during the attack, flew back to Beirut, where Yasser Arafat greeted him with a warm embrace. "I love you as a son!" the PLO leader declared.[3]

A short time later, Salameh orchestrated the hijacking of a Lufthansa airliner. Black September operatives aboard the plane demanded, and secured, the release of the three terrorists who survived the Munich operation. They were flown to Libya in exchange for the airplane, its crew and passengers. When the three survivors reached North African soil, the Libyans greeted them as conquering heroes. After flying to Syria, the men disappeared from the world spotlight.

The attacks during the Munich Olympics proved to be the opening salvo of a yearlong wave of terrorism that took shape across the globe, spurred on by the superheated emotions generated at Munich. Analysis of the patterns and tactics that emerged during these operations suggests that Alon's assassination was linked directly to the post-Munich Shadow War.

The next salvo came five days after what came to be known as the Munich Massacre, on September 10, when an Israeli Mossad agent in Brussels named Zadok Ophir received a phone call from a known informant named Mohammed Rabah.[4] Rabah, an Arab from Morocco, had floated around Europe delving into petty crime from time to time. A year before that call, he had contacted the Israelis from prison to offer tidbits of information related to terrorist groups and attacks. None of it was worth much; Mossad vetted him thoroughly and concluded that Rabah was a fraud and a nut job.

In the phone call that September, Rabah explained breathlessly that he had documented information—a written report—detailing Black September and its organizational structure. Given what had just happened at the Olympics, Ophir agreed to meet Rabah at the Café Prince that same evening.

When Ophir arrived at the appointed hour, the café was empty except for Rabah, who was carrying a briefcase. As the two men sat down, Rabah opened the case, pulled out a revolver, and shot the surprised Mossad agent at point-blank range. Although he had been hit four times, he still tried to draw his own weapon and take out Rabah. Miraculously, Ophir survived the attack, but it served notice that Black September had just declared war on Mossad.

Once again, the tactics looked very similar to the Alon case. The operative used a revolver at point-blank range to try to eliminate his target. As I reviewed this murder attempt in 2006, I began to wonder if perhaps Alon also had known his killer. If so, there was a lot more to Joe Alon than just his service in the Israeli Air Force and his duties as the air attaché in D.C.

After the failed hit on Ophir, Salameh unleashed another operation later that month. Letter bombs were mailed from all over the world to Israeli, Jewish, and American targets. The first casualty occurred in London, when the Israeli agricultural attaché, Dr. Ami Shehori, opened a package that had been mailed from Amsterdam. The explosion killed him instantly.

The letter bomb onslaught continued for weeks. Envelopes and boxes booby-trapped with either cyanide gas or plastic explosives were sent to Israeli leaders and diplomats, Jewish industrialists, and even President Richard Nixon.

At the same time, three Black September terrorists assassinated a Syrian radio journalist in Paris named Khader Kanou. It later came out that the reporter had been an informant for Mossad. Black September was making a point of taking out Israeli secret agents.

In October, Prime Minister Meir met with her senior advisers to discuss the wave of terror. Previously the Israelis had resorted to clandestine assassinations in response to threats to the nation. The first crisis came in the wake of the 1948 War of Independence. Israel next resorted to assassination after a series of cross-border Fedayeen attacks in the mid-1950s staged from Egypt. After Mossad killed the two Egyptian Army officers who had coordinated and supported the incursions, the Fedayeen operations ceased.

In 1962, the Egyptian government hired several German rocket scientists to assist its military in creating a missile system capable of bombarding Israel. To protect its civilian population, Mossad carried out a series of assassinations that eliminated most of the German scientists.

These three crises had set a precedent for the Israeli use of assassination in response to national threats. In 1972, after considering all options, Meir approved a lethal response to this latest wave of attacks. Hit teams, dubbed Wrath of God Squads, would be tasked with taking out the top terrorists who planned and carried out the strikes against Israeli targets. In essence, Mossad would go to war with Black September.

The Israelis deliberated carefully on their opening moves and concluded that the best way to strike back would be to take out Black September's operational leaders in Europe first. They had to be identified, placed under surveillance, and then killed with as little collateral damage as possible.

Rome had long been a hub of terrorist activity. The Italian law enforcement agencies were at best marginally competent. Airport security leaked like a sieve, and Black September had found it easy to smuggle weapons, explosives, and ammunition through the city. Both Salameh and members of the Popular Front for the Liberation of Palestine also had found it relatively easy to hijack airliners staging from Italy.

The Israelis focused on closing this gap first. Through detailed surveillance and intelligence operations, Mossad discovered who served as the Black September commander in Rome. He was an unlikely terrorist named Adel Wael Zwaiter. An erudite intellectual with a passion for literature and art, Zwaiter worked as a translator at the Libyan embassy in Rome. On the surface, he appeared to be a pacifist who floated through the arts and letters scene.

Beneath that cover, however, Zwaiter had provided logistical support and coordination for various Palestinian terror attacks since 1968. As the head of Black September in Rome, he had one of the most strategic positions in Europe.

On October 16, an Israeli assassination team caught Zwaiter in his meagerly furnished apartment. They shot him twelve times at close range with a .22 caliber Beretta pistol.

After his death, the Lebanese media revealed Zwaiter's actual Black September role in Europe. It also revealed that he was Yasser Arafat's cousin.

This first counterblow rocked Black September. The other cell commanders in Europe took notice and began to run scared. In Paris, Dr. Mahmoud Hamshari grew particularly jumpy. A balding, middle-aged Palestinian intellectual, he was a well-known left-wing historian who had emigrated to the City of Lights in 1968 to serve as the PLO's official representative in France. Outwardly he was a soft-spoken pacifist and family man. His cover as an intellectual had served him well for years, but Mossad discovered his real identity and role within Black September.

Hamshari believed wholeheartedly in political assassination as a means to strike blows for the Palestinian cause. He had orchestrated an attempted hit on David Ben-Gurion when the Israeli statesman visited Denmark in 1969. The attempt failed, but that did not discourage Hamshari.

From 1968 to 1972, Hamshari's apartment doubled as a Black September arms depot and hub of terrorist activity. Mossad preoperational surveillance watched late-night comings and goings and concluded that he served as Black September's senior man in Paris.

Killing him would be tricky. He had a family, and the president had expressly forbidden any attacks that could injure the wives or children of men targeted for assassination. As a result, Mossad put together a highly sophisticated operation.

By December 1972, Hamshari had grown exceedingly cautious. Drawing him out was difficult, but Mossad caught a break. An Italian journalist called Hamshari and asked for an interview. When the Black September commander left his apartment, the Mossad surveillance team knew their chance had arrived. Hamshari's wife and children had left the apartment earlier, so it was now empty.

A Mossad team entered the apartment and placed a small amount of plastic explosives under the telephone on his writing desk. A few hours later, when Hamshari returned home, a Mossad officer made a call to Hamshari's number. The doctor answered the phone, and when the voice on the other end of the line asked to speak with him, he confirmed his identity.

The Mossad agent on the phone attracted the attention of another team member, who passed the word that the operation was a go. Another agent with a remote detonator pushed a button and blew the phone to pieces, mortally wounding Hamshari. He died in agony a few days later.

The Israelis had served notice that they were in this fight to win it. Mossad's actions escalated the violence, and Black September unleashed a new wave of attacks in response.

———

Black September's initial counterattack came in a very unlikely place. On December 28, four of its operatives stormed the Israeli embassy in Bangkok, Thailand. Quickly overwhelming the Thai security officers protecting the front gate, they pushed their way inside and seized six Israeli diplomats as hostages. This time, Black September demanded the release of thirty-six terrorists languishing in Israel's prisons in exchange for the diplomats.

The Thai response came fast and furious. They cordoned off the embassy and brought in the Egyptian ambassador, who offered to fly with the terrorists to Cairo if they surrendered the hostages. The terrorists accepted those terms and left the country without bloodshed. Once in Cairo, they took a flight to Beirut, where an enraged Salameh met them. He considered the entire operation a failure that made Black September look weak and foolish. The four agents were never heard from again.

Black September suffered another setback a few weeks later when one of its senior officers ran afoul of a Jordanian army checkpoint. Abu Daoud had been disguised as a Saudi sheikh when suspicious soldiers detained him. Once in custody, he confessed to who he was and revealed he had been on a preoperational surveillance mission in preparation for a full-scale attack on the Jordanian prime minister's office in Amman. The plan, which involved almost twenty Black September operatives, aimed to grab as many senior Jordanian leaders as possible. This was by far one of the most brazen operations Black September had undertaken and was intended to force the Jordanians to release a thousand Fedayeen taken prisoner during the battles.

Daoud confessed again to Jordanian radio and to a British TV news crew. Salameh erupted in anger over this latest failure and recklessly pushed ahead with an operation in Khartoum that carried significant risks of detection.

On the night of March 1, 1973, a team of seven Black September terrorists stormed the Saudi embassy in Khartoum, Sudan, during a party for a departing American diplomat. The terrorists singled out two Americans and a Belgian, executed them, then surrendered. Sudanese police investigating the incident raided the PLO's office in Khartoum and discovered evidence that the top three Palestinian representatives in the country had planned and orchestrated the attack.

This was the first time clear evidence connecting Black September with the PLO gained international attention, and the reaction was swift and harsh. Numerous countries condemned the action, and the Palestinian cause suffered a significant blow.

Salameh seemed to have lost his touch. He tried to make up for the multiple failures with another letter bomb attack, but that failed as well. Later, in the spring of 1973, Black September managed to assassinate a Jewish businessman who had been at the Israeli ambassador's home. Subsequently, Salameh's operatives tried and failed to hijack an Israeli Akria airplane. In Rome, Black September killed an Italian clerk at the El Al office, which did little but inflame world opinion against the Palestinian terrorists.

———————

Cyprus had long been a Dark World battleground, a mix of intelligence agencies, terrorist cells, and Cold War politics that made the little island in the Mediterranean a hotbed for the clandestine war. It was there that Mossad delivered its next blow against Black September.

Hussein Abd el Hir served as the resident senior Black September agent on the island. Politically, he belonged to the PLO's radical faction and freely admitted he was an admirer of the Soviet Union. In fact, KGB agents met with him regularly to discuss joint operations, training, and access to the Soviet military academy. Black September agents received considerable instruction in partisan and guerrilla warfare in the Soviet Union as a result of this association.

In early 1973, Hussein Abd el Hir visited the Soviet embassy. He returned to his hotel late that night, and when he climbed into bed, a Mossad hit team blew him up. When the desk clerk stumbled through the smoke and debris to see what had happened, he discovered that the man's head had been blown into the bathroom's toilet bowl.

Hir's replacement was dispatched at once from Beirut. On April 7, this new operative returned to his room at the Nicosia hotel after meeting with a KGB agent. As he entered his room, he flipped a light switch that had been wired with plastic explosives by another Mossad assassination team. The resulting explosion blew him to pieces.

At the same time, another Israeli team in Paris had been stalking a senior Black September leader named Basil Al-Kubaisi. He had obtained law degrees in both Canada and the United States and had long been an exponent of political assassination. In 1956, he had attempted to kill Iraq's King Faisal with a roadside bomb. Later, he tried to assassinate Golda Meir at JFK Airport in New York by placing a car bomb near the El Al terminal. The weapon was discovered and disarmed shortly before Meir's flight arrived. Not long afterward, he tried and failed once again to kill her in Paris.

On April 6, 1973, a Mossad hit squad discovered him walking back to his apartment after dining at the Café de La Paix in Paris. Just before the assassins struck, a car drove up alongside him. Inside, a beautiful woman made an overture to the professor, who jumped into the car and sped off. The Mossad agent in charge of the assassination team stayed calm, assuming that she was a prostitute and that she would drop the professor back at the original pickup spot when they were finished.

Sure enough, the car rolled back a short time later, and the professor climbed out. The assassins stepped out of the shadows. Al-Kubaisi cried out as he saw them coming, but it was too late. The failed assassin went down mortally wounded with nine close-range bullet holes.

Salameh refused to cede the initiative to the sudden Mossad counterassault. In June, Black September targeted a Mossad agent in Madrid by the name of Baruch Cohen. Cohen had been discovered to be an Israeli agent through a loose network of Palestinian students that he had established in Spain. Some of them served as reliable informants, but ultimately a mole penetrated the circle. He was used to send false intelligence tips to the Israelis before setting up Cohen for assassination. On June 26, Cohen was eating a snack bar when a Black September hit team pumped the Mossad agent's body full of bullets with a silenced pistol at point-blank range. The killers fled to a waiting vehicle and escaped within seconds. Although the police arrived in less than two minutes, by then the trail had gone cold.

As the clandestine war raged, a group of Israeli naval commandos and elite paratroopers trained and rehearsed in Tel Aviv for what would become one of the most devastating blows against the Palestinians. Known as Operation Spring of Youth, Mossad had developed good intelligence that pinpointed the location of no fewer than three senior Black September leaders.

This combined special forces team had been working together since the fall of 1972 for just such an opportunity. Several times, solid intelligence had reached their commander, who wanted to initiate an operation. In each instance, Moshe Dayan refused to give them the green light, fearing the risks outweighed the potential gain.

After the Khartoum massacre, Mossad discovered the location in Beirut of the Popular Democratic Front (PDF), a radical PLO splinter group. Ironically, it was located on the Rue Khartoum. Not far from the headquarters was an apartment complex on the Rue Verdun that Mossad agents had kept under surveillance for months. The operation confirmed that Kamal Nasser, Fatah's chief spokesman, lived on the third floor. One flight down was the apartment of Kamal Adwan, the Black September commander of all operations inside Israeli-held territory. On the sixth floor resided Abu Youssef, Salameh's right-hand man.

This time Dayan approved a raid on all four targets. The Israeli special forces group studied the tactical situation and drew up a daring and aggressive plan with the help of Mossad. The operation began on April Fool's day, 1973, when six Mossad agents flew into Beirut from Europe posing as tourists. At different shorefront hotels, they took rooms with views of the Mediterranean. Over the next few days, the six agents, none of whom knew of the others' presence, carried out further preoperational surveillance on the Rue Verdun and the PDF headquarters. Several also conducted reconnaissance along the nearby beaches. Each also walked to the local Avis lot and rented a large-size car that could hold a number of people. They ended up with three Buick Skylarks, a station wagon, and several more big sedans.

At midnight on April 9, commandos and paratroopers motored ashore in small inflatable boats. Once on the beach, they disguised themselves as hippies or women—a few of the operatives even donned long blond wigs. Then they linked up with the six Mossad agents waiting patiently with their rental cars. Shortly before 1 A.M., the two strike teams set out.

The first group was tasked with blowing up the PDF headquarters. Two commandos sauntered up toward the entrance where two guards stood watch. The guards noticed them, but before they realized anything was amiss, the Israelis produced a pair of silenced Beretta automatic pistols and pumped them both full of lead. They went down, but the attack alerted two more guards watching the street from a nearby jeep. They bailed out of their vehicle and opened fire on the two commandos. One died instantly; the other fell mortally wounded.

At that point, PDF terrorists inside the headquarters grabbed AK-47s and dashed to the windows and balconies. The rest of the Israeli assault force charged up the street, firing as the Palestinians unleashed their automatic weapons. A fierce firefight raged, with the Israelis blasting the upper stories of the PDF building with 81mm mortars and even bazooka rockets. Several commandos fell wounded. One was dragged to safety by a confused Palestinian who thought he had grabbed a comrade.

The Israelis would not be denied. The assault element pressed forward, taking cover behind parked cars until they reached the building's front door. After charging inside, they reached the lobby just as the elevator chimed. Before the door opened, the commandos raked it with bursts from their submachine guns. The elevator became a tomb.

With an Israeli foothold established in the lobby, the Palestinians upstairs did not have a chance. The Israelis quickly wired the first floor with the eighty kilograms (just over 176 pounds) of plastic explosives, then withdrew, carrying their wounded. They piled into the rental cars as the drivers floored the gas pedals. In minutes, they reached the beach just in time to link up with a flight of Israel Defense Forces helicopters dispatched to evacuate the wounded. The rest of the first assault team escaped in the inflatable rafts back to two Israeli missile boats offshore.

Just before the commandos had left the beach, the PDF building blew up. A mushroom cloud of flame spilled up over the Beirut skyline, illuminating the night for miles in all directions. The blast virtually wiped out the PDF faction and killed scores of terrorists.

Meanwhile, the second commando team reached the Rue Verdun about the same time as the attack on the Rue Khartoum began. The men assigned to assassinate the three Black September/Fatah leaders carried with them four photographs. The first three depicted their targets. The fourth was a rare photo of Salameh himself, just in case they stumbled upon him.

The commandos split up into three teams. The first dashed up to the second floor and burst through Adwan's door. Adwan reacted with surprising speed, diving for cover even as he opened fire and wounded one commando. A point-blank gunfight raged inside the apartment, with Adwan's children and wife cowering in the middle of it. Finally, an Israeli paratrooper who had scaled the outside of the building came through a window and killed Adwan with a bullet to the back of his head. The team grabbed its wounded man and started to exit when someone came out of another room down the hallway. The sudden movement caused the commandos to unleash a burst of automatic weapons fire, which ended up killing an elderly Italian woman.

Upstairs, the second assault team blew open Nasser's door and found him sitting at his desk, working on a speech. He reached for an AK-47 propped against the wall next to him, but before he could swing it around and open fire, the Israelis cut him down. Then the commandos raced downstairs to the waiting rental cars. Two out of three targets had been neutralized in a matter of seconds.

The sixth floor presented the greatest challenge. The commando team reached Abu Youssef's apartment door, wired it with plastic explosives, and blew it apart. When they entered, instead of encountering Youssef, they came face-to-face with his sixteen-year-old son. One of the commandos asked him in Arabic where his father was. The terrified boy bolted and escaped to a friend's apartment one floor down.

Then the commandos went room to room, searching for their target. They found him in the master bedroom, still under the covers. His wife had been trying to get a weapon out of the closet, but when the Israelis appeared, she flung herself onto her husband and shielded him with her body. The commandos riddled them both with bullets, leaving the bed soaked crimson with their blood.

Back on the street, the Israelis ran for their waiting getaway cars. Suddenly three Lebanese security vehicles swung around a nearby corner, heading for the apartment complex. The commandos raked them with bullets, knocking out the lead Land Rover. Seconds later, they sped away with Mossad agents. The entire attack had lasted less than five minutes.

———————

Spring of Youth became the signature Israeli success against Black September in 1973. With one blow, the Israelis had taken out a violent and brutal faction of the PLO and assassinated three key Black September/Fatah leaders. It was a tremendous victory.

Yet the victory could have been even bigger. That night, Salameh was sleeping peacefully in a house less than fifty yards from the apartment complex on the Rue Verdun. He took no chances with his personal security; no fewer than seven bodyguards protected him. He also made a point of sleeping at a different place almost every night. When he learned the details of the disaster that had befallen his organization during the night, he viewed the three assassinated leaders with contempt. They had been lax with their security, and he considered them careless amateurs. He had survived to continue the clandestine war.

This brutal underworld killing spree served as the international context of the Alon assassination. Joe had been murdered at a time when Black September was deliberately targeting key Israeli Mossad agents. Mossad's furious response led to an increase in attacks, and as Black September suffered serious losses, Salameh took increasingly daring risks to strike back. The tactics used for these operations all fit the pattern of the Alon assassination. Still, we could find no smoking gun that could directly connect Joe's death to the clandestine war between the Israelis and the Palestinians, just a lot of circumstantial tactical and operational evidence. To solve the case, we would have to find that link, if it existed.

CHAPTER FOURTEEN
UNBRIDLED VENGEANCE

Spring and Summer, 1973

Through the spring and summer of 1973, the Israelis increased their efforts to destroy Black September, and the clandestine war came to its bloody climax.

In the days after Operation Spring of Youth, a senior Black September commander named Abu Ziad Mokhsi heard a radio report from Beirut that the Israelis had launched a commando raid on his organization's senior leadership. He had been living in Athens when the news broke, and up until then he had been very careful to mask his movements. He had stayed in his hotel room as much as possible and went out only when he absolutely had to. But when he heard the radio report, he lost his composure and bolted to the nearest newspaper stand. He bought several papers and was engrossed in reading them when a large Greek man blocked his path. Ziad Mokhsi tried to get around him, but the man barred his path again. It took an annoyed Ziad Mokhsi several moments to disentangle himself from the rude man.

That orchestrated delay gave a Mossad hit squad just enough time to plant a bomb in Ziad Mokhsi's hotel room in the Aristides Hotel. When he returned, the Israelis called him to confirm he was actually on-site. Then they detonated a remote IED. The Wrath of God Squads could scratch another Black September leader off their list.

The Israelis had scored some impressive victories, but they were not about to let go of their growing stranglehold on Black September. Mossad kept the tempo of targeted assassinations on pace to deter future attacks. For several years, Mossad had pursued a deadly terrorist named Mohammed Boudia, an Algerian who had cut his teeth during his country's war of liberation against France. A specialist in sabotage, he had been caught and imprisoned in France for three years. When the war ended in 1962, the French released him, and he returned to Algeria briefly. After a coup, he went into exile in France, where the KGB recruited him and sent him to the Soviet Union for further training. He emerged a capable and very elusive master of the Shadow War. In the years that followed, he masterminded attacks on oil refineries in Trieste and Rotterdam for the Popular Front for the Liberation of Palestine.

In 1972, Mossad picked up intelligence that suggested Boudia had split with the PFLP and joined Ali Hassan Salameh as Black September's head of operations in France. Wanted by the Italians, Dutch, and Swiss, he seemed to live a charmed life in France, where the authorities did not have much heart to pursue him. That left him free to carry out smuggling and arms-running operations, and he later planned the assassination of the Syrian radio journalist Khader Kanou.

Boudia was typical of the Black September leaders of the era: erudite, artistic, and intellectual. His outward persona suggested a man who loved the arts. Mossad considered him the most dangerous Black September operative in Europe after Salameh.

In May 1973, the Israelis dispatched a team of agents to Paris to track down Boudia. They knew he had one key weakness: a penchant for women. The Mossad team decided to watch several prominent females who were part of the left-wing intelligentsia in Paris, hoping that perhaps Boudia would pay one a visit.

The ploy worked. With great tactical patience, the surveillance operation picked up Boudia's trail when he showed up at a visiting female law professor's apartment. They prepared to strike as soon as he left the building, but he never reappeared. The hit squad could not figure out how he had slipped away.

They maintained a vigil on the apartment for the next month and watched Boudia arrive multiple times. Yet he never exited the building. Several blond and brunette females usually left for work or errands or breakfast in the postdawn hours, but the surveillance team never detected Boudia's departure.

Finally the Israeli agents figured out what was going on. Boudia had been a theater manager and actor in Algeria. After his amorous encounters with the law professor, he would dress in drag and slip away every morning with none of the Mossad operatives the wiser.

Catching him became a priority. Fragments of information from various sources indicated that he was about to launch a series of attacks on Israeli embassies around Europe. To carry them out, he and Black September had been actively forming alliances with other radical left-wing groups throughout the Old World.

A tip led the surveillance team to stake out a Métro station in the Paris subway system. For days they studied the crowds until they finally spotted him, heavily disguised at the Étoile station beneath the Arc de Triomphe—Boudia was a true master of

theatrical makeup, and the team almost missed him. Nevertheless, they followed his trail and watched him get into a car.
When the agents ran his tags, they were astonished to discover
that this ultra-careful terrorist had registered the vehicle in his
own name.

The car became Boudia's liability. On June 28, he parked it in
Paris's famed Latin Quarter near another of his lovers' apartments. While he was upstairs, the Mossad team wired his little
sedan with explosives. The next morning, when he left the
woman's apartment, he approached his car very carefully. He
checked the wheels, then bent low and studied the chassis. After
he climbed inside, the Wrath of God Squad detonated the bomb
and watched as the most dangerous man in Europe burned inside
his metal Achilles' heel.[1]

Three nights later, Joe Alon was gunned down in the front
yard of his Trent Street house. Coming so quickly after Boudia's
assassination, had Joe's killing been a retaliatory strike? The July
5, 1973 Cairo radio broadcast after the killing of Boudia claimed
Joe's killing was in retaliation for Boudia's death. If Joe's assassination had been part of the clandestine war between Black September and Israel, it would not be the end. Instead, it was just one
episode in a lengthy list of killings that continued long after his
death in my hometown that predawn July morning.

———————

In July 1973, the Israelis developed intelligence suggesting that
Salameh and Black September were about to launch an attack of
some kind in Sweden. Mossad dispatched additional assets to
northern Europe, and through a series of surveillance operations,
several agents on the ground thought they had located Salameh
himself in Lillehammer, Norway.

On July 21, a Wrath of God squad tailed Salameh to a local movie theater, where he watched a World War II espionage film called *Where Eagles Dare* with a beautiful blonde Norwegian. After the show, the two exited the theater and began walking home.

The two-man hit team struck with savage speed. They rolled up in a white Mazda behind the couple, and the Mossad agents went after their target. Salameh spun around just in time to see the agents draw their .22 caliber Berettas. "No!" he shouted. The assassins pumped his thin body full of bullets, then fled back to the waiting car. They left him bleeding out in the street while the woman wailed for help.

Days later, Mossad discovered that the agents had made a grievous error. The man killed that night was not Salameh at all but a struggling Moroccan waiter who had emigrated to Norway in search of a job and a better life. He had married a local woman and was just starting a family. His wife, the blonde who cried over his body as his lifeblood drained out, was seven months pregnant.

If that were not bad enough, the Norwegian authorities caught and jailed six of the Israeli agents involved in the assassination. One of them was captured at an Israeli diplomat's apartment, which established a clear link between the agents and the Israeli government. Under interrogation, two of the most junior and inexperienced agents broke. They not only provided details of the Lillehammer operation but also supplied vast amounts of information related to how Mossad functioned in Europe. Their revelations forced the Israelis to withdraw agents, abandon safe houses, extract informants, and change phone numbers all over the continent. Mossad's ability to chase Black September terrorists had been dealt a crippling blow.

Worse, when the international news media learned what had happened in Norway, there was a mass outpouring of outrage and hostile press toward the Israelis. Diplomatic relations between the Jewish state and much of Europe soured. Golda Meir, who had recognized the consequences should these assassinations ever come to light, called off the pursuit of Black September's last surviving leaders, at least for the time being.

That fall, the Syrians and Egyptians launched their surprise attack on Israel, leading to the Yom Kippur War. Outnumbered, facing new Soviet technology that cost the Israeli Air Force dearly, the Israelis found themselves fighting for the very survival of their nation. They committed all efforts, both conventional and covert, to the new war. The allegations of intelligence failures leading up to Yom Kippur may have given the remaining Black September leaders breathing space to escape and continue their plotting, but the Israelis did not forget. It took them years, but eventually they settled the score that started at Munich. After Lillehammer, Abu Iyad and Ali Hassan Salameh were living on borrowed time.

After the assassinations and counterassassinations of 1973, Black September virtually collapsed. Yet the stature of Salameh—the Red Prince—had risen ever higher in Arafat's mind, probably due to his loyalty and personal connection to the Palestine Liberation Organization leader. This development rankled Abu Iyad. A struggle for power broke out until Abu Iyad finally gave Arafat an ultimatum: Salameh or him. The PLO leader chose Salameh and made him the head of his personal security detail in 1974.

That year, Arafat flew to New York to address the United Nations.[2] He strode into the main chamber on November 13 carrying an olive branch in one hand and a gun in the other. Before he even spoke, the UN delegations broke into applause that rose to a tremendous crescendo.

Salameh traveled with Arafat to New York and virtually never left his side. As the head of his security team, he worked closely with the New York Police Department. A known terrorist, one of the world's most wanted men, had come to the United States with the approval, foreknowledge, and assistance of the U.S. government. Something clearly was not right with that scenario. In the early 1990s, when I first discovered that Salameh had come to this country, it bothered me. Clearly someone had worked behind the scenes at the State Department to allow such a thing to happen, but I could not discover why or who.

Five years after Salameh's visit to the United States, in January 1979, the Israelis finally caught up to the Red Prince. After an effective preoperational surveillance mission, Mossad determined that he had let his guard down. He had married Georgina Rizak, a beautiful Christian Lebanese woman and former Miss Universe, who was now pregnant.[3] Together, they lived in an apartment in Snoubra, one of Beirut's nicer districts. He seemed to have forgotten all of the tricks he had used to evade the Wrath of God Squads in 1973. Salameh had traded the constant movement and paranoia of a master terrorist for domestic harmony. As the Mossad team observed him, they quickly discovered he had sunk into a routine. They soon figured out when and where Salameh would go during his days and mapped out the streets he frequented the most.

On January 22, the Red Prince climbed into a tan Chevrolet station wagon occupied by two bodyguards and was driven down

the Rue Verdun, followed by a Land Rover with two more bodyguards. His vehicle turned onto the Rue Madame Curie and
passed what looked to be an average blue Volkswagen parked by
the curb. From a window overlooking the street, a female Mossad
agent, later identified as Erika Chambers, pressed a remote control in her hand and watched the Volkswagen explode. The full
force of the blast broadsided Salameh's station wagon. In a flash,
the original bomb triggered the Chevy's gas tank, and the vehicle
blew up. Flames shot up through the neighborhood as debris—
including body parts—rained down. Salameh and his four-man
bodyguard detail were killed.

———————

Abu Iyad survived the clandestine war of the 1970s, wrote a book
about his experiences,[4] and settled in Tunis after the 1982 PLO
withdrawal from Lebanon. In his later years, his tone moderated,
and he began to advocate for a face-to-face dialogue with Israel.
Although Arafat eased him out of his inner circle in the 1970s,
Abu Iyad remained personally loyal to the PLO chief. In 1991, he
was assassinated in Tunis. Most sources suggest he was killed either by an agent loyal to the terrorist Abu Nidal or by a faction
within the PLO. However, evidence suggests that the Israelis finished him off with a commando team that slipped ashore in rub-
ber inflatable boats in an operation reminiscent of the Spring of
Youth eighteen years before.

     With the assassination of Abu Iyad in 1991, the last of the
Black September leaders had been wiped out. The loop had been
closed, and it seemed that by the early 1990s, except for Arafat
himself, no one was left alive who could confirm or deny a Black
September role in Joe Alon's death.

A few years after Abu Iyad fell to an assassin's bullets, my superiors within the DSS assigned me to guard Yasser Arafat when he returned to New York to speak at the UN. We provided close security for him and watched as various dignitaries and businessmen came to his hotel room to kiss his ring. Most brought bundles of cash that they deposited in a big garbage can by the hotel room door.

Arafat spent his time in New York either in his hotel room or at meetings. Watching him, I was struck by the reverence all his visitors showered on the Palestinian leader. I also noticed that his personal security detail was almost as good as our DSS agents. Thorough, vigilant, and fiercely loyal to Arafat, their professionalism shone through in all of their actions and tactics. Once, I recalled watching dinner arrive in the hotel room. When Arafat's plate was served, one of his bodyguards suddenly stepped forward, grabbed it, and switched it with the man seated next to his boss. As he did so, the security agent glanced up at me and caught my expression of surprise. He gave me a sly smile then melted away from the table. If Arafat's food had been poisoned, the guest sitting next to him would have ingested it.

Although Salameh had long been in his grave, his legacy was alive in that room. He was the first one to truly professionalize Arafat's personal protection. Fatah-17 had grown into a security force that ranked as one of the best I had ever seen during my career in the DSS.

As we worked with them, I wanted to ask Arafat about Salameh and the clandestine war. While I was working with the DSS, my thoughts sometimes returned to Black September, and I wondered if Abu Iyad and Salameh had had anything to do with Joe's death. There was not any evidence, but it somehow seemed to fit. I thought perhaps that, after all these years, Arafat might talk about it. But I never found the right moment to question the Palestinian leader.

To this day, I kick myself for not approaching him. Instead, I did my job and continued to wonder if Black September really had had a role in Alon's death. Opportunities like that one come along only once; that I let it slip away has haunted me ever since. Of course, Arafat probably never would have told me—an agent of the U.S. government—anything. Still, he might have thrown me some tidbit that would have shed light on this case.

Instead, in 2006, as I sat down to study the patterns, motives, and operational tactics used by Black September, it was very clear that similarities existed between them and Joe Alon's killers. His killers knew who Joe was, what he looked like, where he lived, and where he would be the night of the murder. Joe was the perfect target: an IAF pilot inside America. Such information takes time and connections to develop. Black September's operatives always did their homework before a mission. Whoever killed Alon had been similarly thorough.

The weapons Black September used for assassination attempts matched almost perfectly with how Joe was killed. The group never relied on a long-range shot by a sharpshooting sniper staring at his target through the crosshairs of a telescopic sight. Instead, their hit teams always got in close and emptied a revolver into their victim at point-blank range.

The attempted assassination of Mossad agent Zadok Ophir in Belgium fit this pattern perfectly. So did the murder of Baruch Cohen in Spain, although in that instance the gunmen used a silenced pistol instead of a revolver. That was probably an operational necessity, given the public nature of the hit.

As I contemplated the similarities, I came back to the fact that in both these other cases, the targeted Mossad agent had been in contact with Black September personnel. Ophir knew Mohammed Rabah personally. In Spain, Cohen had penetrated a group of Palestinian students with Black September ties. In each case, the Mossad agent was betrayed and shot.

The IAF was always hypervigilant—borderline paranoid—about security. Photos of its pilots were rarely published, and press reports on the aviators rarely mentioned their full names. It would not have been easy for Black September to discover who Joe was, even though he lived in an unsecure neighborhood at the time of the murder.

When he first met Colonel Joe Alon in the Pentagon, Merrill McPeak assumed that this civilian-attired air attaché was a spy as well as an IAF officer. Could Joe really have been working for Mossad while in the United States? If so, most likely he would have been reporting on the U.S. military. But what if he had some other mission in the United States, one that might explain why the Israelis were so quick to turn their back on him and try to bury the case?

In light of the history and context of the time, this idea appeared at least as plausible as Dvora's conspiracy theory. The challenge I faced now was trying to figure out if there was anything to this line of thought.

In 2007, as work load and family life allowed, I would follow a lead here and there, talk to Ed, and discuss loose ends. I renewed my efforts with Joe's daughters. I asked them if they had seen, heard, or suspected that their father might have been working for

Mossad. Those questions triggered two memories that raised interesting possibilities.

Yola recalled that in the weeks before the murder, she had discovered an odd-looking device on the top shelf of a bookcase inside the Trent Street house.[5] She was climbing up to look at birthday cards when she discovered the device. I asked her to describe it for me, and she recalled it was about twelve centimeters long by nine centimeters wide (about four inches by four-and-three-quarter inches). It was not very thick—only two centimeters (about three-quarters of an inch). Across the top were several rows of small circular or square buttons—Yola could not remember exactly—four or five to each row. The device was solid black.

I took this description to an old acquaintance of mine who had served in the American intelligence community during the 1980s and 1990s. Retired now, he proved more than willing to help me figure out what the device might have been.[6]

"Sounds like an ancient SRAC," he told me. SRAC stands for "short-range agent communication" equipment. He went on to explain that the buttons were most likely letters that used a stylus to punch out a very short, coded message that would be sent to a nearby receiving unit. The agent using this device had either to travel to a location near that unit or to have one prepositioned close by. At the same time, there had to be another agent using the receiving device in order to get the transmission.

While living in Bethesda, Joe Alon possessed a key piece of equipment used by intelligence agents. SRAC equipment was not standard issue to Israeli diplomats or air force officers. Agents and handlers, or agents and their own network of assets, used this type of communication equipment to pass encrypted messages. I wished I had a more detailed description of the device to confirm that it really was an SRAC, but Yola provided all that she could remember.[7]

The daughters also recalled one other interesting point that suggested Joe had some sort of contact with the U.S. intelligence community. Every few weeks, an American in civilian clothes arrived on Saturday morning. He brought doughnuts for the girls and Dvora, then he and Joe would go talk quietly behind a closed door. Dvora always made sure the girls left the two men alone.[8]

As I considered these two puzzle pieces, Ed and I finally caught a major break in the case.

CHAPTER FIFTEEN
COMING INTO FOCUS

June 2006

I sent a request to the Montgomery County Police Alumni Association asking that anyone with knowledge of the Alon case contact me. Through the association, I developed some excellent contacts, which prompted me to place an ad in the newsletter in hopes of casting a wider net. Ed Golian responded the next day. In March 2009, we also heard from Detective Kenny McGee of the Montgomery County Police, one of the detectives on the scene that night.

Detective McGee had been among the first to respond the night Alon was murdered. The big ambulance's flashing lights bathed the scene in a reddish glow. And as McGee stood on the driveway, a man drove up, got out of his car, and walked up to the scene.

It was General Mordechai Gur. McGee remembers him vividly. He looked absolutely shocked, almost dazed, as he stared at the blood staining the front yard. McGee went over to talk to him and find out if he might have anything of value to share. He did.

The general told McGee explicitly that Colonel Joseph Alon was a Mossad agent using his diplomatic status as a military attaché as his cover. Gur requested that this information be kept quiet and undocumented.[1] It never was. In fact, the official police report states the opposite: that Joe was not Mossad.[2]

McGee worked the case with the FBI for several months. When no headway was made, the Montgomery County Police Department reassigned him to other cases. Months after he was taken off the case, an FBI associate who had worked with him on the Alon murder tipped him off as to the killer and his fate. McGee said that the FBI agent told him that the Israelis had followed the murderer to Canada, from where he had fled to Egypt and went into hiding. Mossad located him there and sent a hit squad after him. The squad raided his home, killing not only Joe's murderer but his entire family.

The FBI agent told McGee not to speak of this to anyone and not to document anything. The matter was dropped; case closed. Yet McGee always wondered if that information was any good. Something bothered him about it; it did not ring true.

It did not seem to ring true to me either. Back in the 1970s, through the entire Shadow War, both Black September and Mossad took pains to avoid harming the families of their targets. In that respect anyway, the assassins on both sides still played a gentleman's game. In all the violence that spread across three continents after Munich, only Abu Youssef's wife had been killed.

Aside from the story of how the murderer was tracked and killed, McGee's information confirmed what I had begun to suspect: Joe Alon had come to the United States in the early 1970s on his last tour as an Israeli Air Force officer. After the completion of his duty in D.C., he would have retired. Like so many Israel Defense Forces officers, he probably had been recruited by

Mossad and had a career in the intelligence community waiting for him once he separated from the military. The United States was probably one of his first assignments, if not his first, for his new bosses within Mossad.

I could not help but to think back to Yola and Rachel's story about their meeting with General Gur shortly before his death. He told them nothing and went to his grave without helping his old comrade's children find the closure they so desperately needed. Part of me could not help but despise the man for that.

But for that moment of weakness in July 1973, as he stared at the crime scene and talked to McGee, we may never have been able to confirm Joe's dual role in America. Once the general regained his composure, however, he never made such a revelation again.

———————

Two pieces of evidence—McGee's memory and Yola's recollection of what could have been a communications device used by spies of the era—suggested that Joe Alon had been an intelligence officer. We needed to figure out his role in the clandestine war—if he had one. Clearly, his duties as the air force attaché held tremendous importance, both to the Israelis and to the United States. He was a critical liaison with the USAF, the Pentagon, and the CIA. The next step was to find out if, as a Mossad agent, his responsibilities that dovetailed with that role were completely different.

In Maryland, this development in the case energized Ed as much as it did me. He continued working through official channels to try to find more documentation on the case. In the process, he was tipped off that the FBI office in New York City might have some promising tidbits on Joe's murder. This gave us both pause. Why would there be anything related to Joe in the

New York field office's files? To our knowledge, he had never visited New York.

Determined to leave no stone unturned, Ed and Joe Mudano traveled to New York and began to sift through piles of documents three decades old. It was laborious work, but it paid off. In one long-forgotten memo, Ed discovered that the New York office had cultivated an informant who had taken part in the plot to kill Golda Meir at John F. Kennedy Airport. This was Basil Al-Kubaisi's operation, and the informant was part of the Black September presence in the Big Apple. He had worked with notorious Black September terrorist Khalid Al-Jawary, who had been deeply involved in the JFK plot. Al-Jawary's mission in the United States in the 1970s had been to identify potential targets for Black September attacks. He had also built the bombs placed at the airport.

The informant had grown disaffected with Al-Jawary and Black September, and later testified against them, which helped put his former associate behind bars. In return, the government discreetly relocated him from the New York City area. Ed discovered he was still alive and living under an assumed name in the American Southeast.

The FBI agents working the MURDA case back in Baltimore had no idea the New York field office had developed a source within the stateside Black September network. Stan did not know either. It was a stone that had been left unturned thirty-five years before. At last, we had a fresh lead to track down. I eagerly awaited news from Ed and Joe, who had flown to the former informant's current home and spent a day talking with him at his residence.

During the interview, Ed showed the informant a photo of Joe Alon. The aging Black September operative recognized him at once, although he did not know his name. "I met with him twice in New York City," the source told Ed. Each time he was sent to rendezvous with the Israeli, he had been told to bring along a beautiful woman, who was also a Black September asset. The Palestinians may have known of Joe's weakness for good-looking women, and these meetings were designed, in part, to take advantage of that weakness.

The source also mentioned that Al-Jawary had met with Joe at least once in New York.[3]

The fact that the man assigned to scope out stateside targets for Black September had a relationship with a murdered Israeli diplomat was surprising. Given how the other Mossad agents were hit in Europe, this tidbit of information all but confirmed that he had been assassinated by the terrorist arm of the Palestine Liberation Organization.

This revelation led us to conclude that Joe was trying to cultivate an intelligence source within Black September's New York cell. He might have thought these meetings were initial contact points, but the people he met with were playing a very different game. They were cultivating him—as a target. This is how Black September learned who Joe Alon was, and it probably allowed the group to set up the preoperational surveillance and intelligence effort that resulted in his death.

The process could not have been quick. Black September's stateside network surely must have spent months developing intelligence on Joe's patterns and travels. But once they figured out that he was not just a Mossad agent but the air attaché at the Israeli embassy, a war hero, and a founding member of the IAF, there was no way Abu Iyad or Ali Hassan Salameh could have passed up a chance to kill him. He was simply too symbolic a target, no matter the risks. No Palestinian terrorist organization had ever been able to kill one of the hated pilots of the IAF. These were the men who flew with impunity over the refugee camps and training centers in Lebanon, bombing and rocketing at will. His murder would have sent shock waves through the IAF and raised the morale of Palestinians everywhere.

Joe's role in New York also made sense with regard to how the Israelis reacted to his assassination. He had been burned by a mole or snared by Black September in a very clever trap. Either General Gur had ordered Joe to infiltrate the Black September network, or he knew of his activities. Because of his comment to Dvora the night of the murder—when he wondered why it had been Joe, not he, who had been murdered—it seems possible Gur had orchestrated the operation.

Given the fragility of the military alliance between Israel and the United States in 1973, it is not surprising that Joe's comrades and friends quickly swept his murder under the carpet. He was a spy functioning in a friendly country; had the FBI discovered this fact, it could have been catastrophic. Relations between Israel and the United States would surely have soured at a critical time when the IDF depended on U.S. military aid. Alon's day job put him square in the middle between the IDF and the U.S. Air Force, a position that required considerable tact and charm. He served as the link between the two militaries, and in that role he was privileged to see a great deal about how the USAF functioned.

Imagine if the United States learned such a key figure in a budding relationship with Israel was actually trying to build an espionage network along the eastern seaboard. To keep that from happening, the Israelis buried Joe Alon, and the government did its best to forget him and his assassination. That was why Dvora and her daughters could never learn the truth.

Years after Alon's murder, in the 1980s when I first joined the Diplomatic Security Service, U.S. relations with Israel were frosty at best. Jonathan Pollard, a civilian contractor who worked for U.S. Naval intelligence, had sold a staggering amount of classified material to the Israelis until he was finally caught in 1985. By the time the FBI closed in on him, the damage had global ramifications. His betrayal had burned agents, operations, and entire networks. Few other spies have inflicted as much harm on U.S. intelligence agencies and its defense community as Pollard did. When the case came to light, it was suspected that the Israelis might have taken some of that information and traded it to the Soviets in exchange for the release of several key Jewish scientists. The special connection that Joe Alon had helped to establish between the United States and the Jewish state suffered serious harm.

Joe might not have been spying on the USAF during his time in the States, but the fact that such an important individual was living a double life as an intelligence agent might have tipped the scales against Israel at a critical time. Only a few months after Alon's death, the United States came to Israel's rescue during the Yom Kippur War. Had it not been for the U.S. response and its massive resupply effort, the IDF never would have survived the combined Arab surprise attack. A lot was riding on Joe Alon dying a martyr's death and being remembered by all as simply an aviator turned diplomat.

———

In the spring of 2009, after we learned of Joe's double life in America, Ed and I discussed where to take the investigation. We had our suspect organization, how and why Joe had been targeted, and the actual mechanics of the assassination. Armed with these new leads, we decided to see if we could identify who gave the order to kill Joe and who carried out the attack. Ed went to work trying to secure an opportunity to interview.

After Abu Iyad died in 1991, Al-Jawary flew from Iraq to his funeral. His plane stopped in Rome, where authorities there detained him for traveling on a fake passport. The Italians handed him over to the FBI, and he was convicted in Brooklyn for building the car bombs that were used in the JFK Airport assassination attempt on Golda Meir. He was sentenced to thirty years in prison and was serving his term in a federal super-maximum security facility. Trying to get an interview or have the FBI ask him questions about the Alon case was not going to be an easy task. As Ed worked that angle, I worked an international slant that I thought might serve us very well.

During my career with the DSS, I spent a lot of time in Beirut working with agents and assets in Lebanon. That part of my career culminated in 1994, when we discovered Hasan Izz-Al-Din was making a weekly visit to a lady friend at an apartment complex not far from the U.S. Embassy in Beirut. We had been after him for years, and this looked like the choice opportunity to nab him in a "rendition"-style operation and get him to the United States, where he would stand trial for his crimes.

Izz-Al-Din's crimes were numerous and bloody. As a senior member of the Iranian-backed terrorist organization Hezbollah, he had worked closely with Hezbollah operations chief Imad Mugniyah on numerous attacks on American targets. Their most spectacular blow against the United States came in 1983, when the group plotted and executed the bombing of the American embassy in Beirut, an attack that coincided with a meeting of top CIA agents in the region and resulted in the death of Near East director Robert Ames and seven other agency officers. A few months later, Izz-Al-Din and Mugniyah orchestrated the truck bombing attack on the U.S. Marine barracks in Beirut, killing 241

Americans. The two men had more blood on their hands than any other terrorists of the era.

If we could insert a team of DSS agents through the U.S. Embassy into Beirut, we figured we might be able to snatch him at his girlfriend's apartment, get him back to the embassy, and fly him out of the country. Such a mission was fraught with risks. Local authorities could not know what we were doing. The Lebanese police and security agencies were riddled with Hezbollah informants and sympathizers. Besides, they would not have been predisposed to allow the United States to essentially kidnap a Lebanese citizen, no matter how evil he was.

The extraction had to be done totally under the radar of the local authorities. This meant that if something went wrong, the agents would be totally exposed in a hostile city. I thought of Lillehammer and the assassination of the Moroccan waiter and how its repercussions had tarnished Israel. I thought of Operation Spring of Youth and how one Israeli commando was shot and wounded during the assassinations in the apartment complex on the Rue Verdun.

In the end, I could not risk our agents, who were personal friends of mine. The operation would have put them in grave peril if anything went wrong. Experience had taught me that in the clandestine world, operations rarely went as planned. Izz-Al-Din was never caught, and the decision I made is one that has haunted me ever since.

Nevertheless, in the years that followed, I maintained my contacts and assets on the ground in Lebanon. When I left the DSS and became the vice president for counterterrorism at Strategic Forecasting, I continued to keep in touch with those old friends via electronic dead drops.

Back in Joe Alon's day, a dead drop was a mutually agreed-on physical location. There agents and spies would place documents, orders, or other vital information at designated times. It was a means to pass intelligence or communicate. With the advent of the digital age, dead drops have migrated to the Internet. Two agents who want to communicate via email do not need to send messages back and forth to each other. Doing so would leave an electronic trail that can be traced and retrieved. Instead, an email address is set up with a mutually agreed-on password that both agents possess. When they want to communicate, they compose an email, then save it to the Drafts folder. Because the message is never sent, there is no electronic footprint that can attract other agencies or governments. This simple and elegant solution allows agents and assets to stay in constant touch, no matter where they are in the world. This is how I maintained my connection with my sources in Lebanon while at Stratfor.

I posted a message in the Drafts folder of one of my electronic dead drops. My old friend on the other side of the world picked it up only a few days later and agreed to help out.

To this day, negotiating the murky underworld in Beirut is a dangerous game. One slip and people disappear. I had asked my contact to reach out to anyone he knew in Lebanon who had once worked with the senior Black September leadership and to cautiously begin asking around about the Alon murder.

My source already had relationships with three aging members of Black September and the Palestine Liberation Organization. To protect their lives, I cannot name them within these pages, but all three were highly placed in the two organizations and shared personal relationships with Ali Hassan Salameh, Yasser Arafat, and Abu Iyad. When my Beirut contact reached out to them, he had to tread very carefully so as not to reveal the true na-

ture of our investigation. Instead, his interest was purely historical, he maintained.

Among the first nuggets of information he brought back to
me was the fact that Black September documented every operation it launched between 1970 and 1974. In the process, its
members interviewed hundreds of Jordanian, Palestinian,
Lebanese, and Syrian operatives and sympathizers. After each
mission, the interviews were compiled into a comprehensive,
detailed report typed up on the same typewriter in Beirut. No
copies were made. The original material was then stored in a
specially prepared safe that served as Black September's historical archive. The safe required two keys to open, one of which
was in Arafat's possession. The other was kept by the head of
the Palestinian Research Institute.

According to my contact's informant, the Israelis captured the
safe during the invasion of Lebanon in 1982. The IDF raided the
Palestinian Research Institute and hauled away the entire library.
The Black September documents became the property of the Hebrew University in Jerusalem.

I did my best to confirm the location of those files. I asked
one of Stratfor's leading Israeli analysts if he knew anyone at the
university. He did not, but did know four professors who specialized in radical Islamic groups. Three held positions at Tel Aviv
University; one had worked closely with the IDF for almost three
decades. The other taught at Haifa University. Our analyst contacted all four in search of the Black September archive and safe.

None of the four admitted to knowing anything about such
material, and all doubted that they were stored at Hebrew University. One reported back that if the IDF had indeed captured
such files, they would be jealously guarded by Israel's intelligence
community. Bottom line: We could forget about this avenue of

investigation. This was a particularly bitter pill to swallow; the mission reports from the clandestine war might have included one on the Alon assassination that might have helped us identify who ordered, planned, and executed the assassination.

If the Black September files really were in Israeli hands, it underscored the level of deception and secrecy they maintained around Joe Alon's murder. The family's repeated requests for information had resulted in the release of the barest of details, despite the court case the daughters brought against the Israeli government. If the secondary source in Beirut was right—and he was perfectly placed to know exactly what had happened to the safe—the Israelis might have known of Black September's role in the Alon assassination since 1982. That thought and the shocking treatment of Joe's family over the years made me even more determined to help Rachel and Yola find justice and closure.

While waiting for more details from my Beirut contact, I received a bolt from the blue. Two associates of mine who work in the media industry contacted me with information that led to yet another twist in the Alon case. This time, instead of aging memories and human sources, the latest break in the case came from no less of a place than the U.S. National Archives.

CHAPTER SIXTEEN

THE CIA'S INVOLVEMENT

2008

The documents were scattered around my desk at home. The National Archives periodically declassifies information deemed obsolete or sanitized. In this instance, the agency released a raft of formerly classified briefings delivered to members of Congress by the FBI and CIA. These briefings, which took place in the late 1970s behind closed doors, detailed various terrorist threats and operations against U.S. targets at home and abroad. Through the diligent efforts of Adam Goldman and Randy Herschaft of the Associated Press, who had also been researching Joe's killing, the memo was data mined from the files. As I read through the pertinent documents, I read the incredible admission made by the agency on August 4, 1978.

```
The next briefing was on the assassination of
Israeli air attaché to the U.S. Josef [sic] Alon
in July 1973. . . . It was noted that information
that came to our attention years after the
```

```
assassination indicated that Fatah/Black
September was "probably" responsible for the
murder, and that a two man hit team had entered
the U.S. specifically to carry it out and had
left immediately afterwards.¹
```

The Central Intelligence Agency knew Black September had carried out the assassination of Joe Alon. This revelation came a year after the case had been closed and the evidence in FBI hands destroyed. What is more, the CIA had learned the details of the assassination operation directly from a "senior Fedayeen official." A highly placed CIA informant—within the Palestine Liberation Organization, Fatah, or Black September; the documents did not specify—had revealed that the assassination had been carried out by two Arab students who had come into the country just prior to the mission. They had entered the United States via Canada on Lebanese or Cypriot passports, then traveled to Washington, D.C., where they stayed with other Palestinian students in the area. An Arab professor teaching at a university in the D.C. area took part in the pre-mission logistical operation. There was also references in the authors' notes from old FBI Baltimore teletypes indicating that alleged surveillances of Alon were carried out by a group of students from a specific D.C. university that shall be unnamed due to legal reasons. The professor was the one who had rented the white sedan and acquired the weapons to be used by the student assassins. The revolvers were placed in the trunk and the car prepositioned for the operation. The students then were driven to its location on the night of the murder.

The getaway car was abandoned somewhere after the hit team killed Joe, as were the weapons. The team did an outstanding job in this regard. The car was never located. The next day, the young assassins either flew out of the country via Dulles Airport or used another rental car to drive across the country, where they departed the United States from a West Coast airport.[2]

————————

If this information was accurate, Alon's two murderers might still be at large, which meant that we still had a chance of securing justice for Rachel and Yola. I worked to track down the "senior Fedayeen official." Fortunately, my media associates had already done much of the legwork. Included in my stack of documents were a series of cables and diplomatic telegrams that had passed between the State Department and the U.S. Embassy in Beirut. Most of the material they contained was mundane, boring government matters. However, one cable sent from Beirut to Washington provided the proverbial smoking gun.

In November 1974, as Yasser Arafat prepared to travel to New York to give his famous address to the United Nations, U.S. Embassy "officials" met with a key member of Arafat's entourage. Ostensibly, the meeting was to discuss security issues and concerns for the Palestine Liberation Organization leader while he visited the United States. However, the conversation went well beyond that, as the cable reported.

```
1. In course of Nov 11 discussions with Fatah's
   "Ali Hassan Salameh" RE travel of Arafat and
   Co. . . . EMBOFF [embassy official] took
   opportunity to inquire RE BSO [Black
   September] Chief Abu Iyad. Salameh indicated
   PLO/Fatah leadership remains ignorant of Abu
   Iyad's whereabouts and is actively trying to
   find out where he is at present. He said, "Abu
```

Iyad will have lots of questions to answer when we find him." Admitting that persons arrested in Morocco included several of Abu Iyad's "boys," Salameh said he found reports that their targets included Arab leaders other than King Hussein "hard to believe." At same time, he remarked with apparent bitterness that Qadafi "corrupts every one of us he touches."

2. Salameh thought that Abu Iyad, when he finally surfaces, would probably be able to explain his role in the Rabat Affair to Arafat's satisfaction but if he died [Abu Iyad] would emerge from it as "hero" in Fedayeen eyes. While most Palestinians still regard King Hussein as "fair game" for future assassination attempts, said Salameh, his murder at Rabat would have been "disaster" for the Palestinian cause, since it would have thrown summit conference into confusion, prevented achievement of valuable political gains won by PLO at Rabat, and caused Arafat to appear at UNGA [UN General Assembly] "with Hussein's blood on his hands." "We assassinated Hussein politically in Rabat," Salameh remarked, "and that should have given enough satisfaction to Abu Iyad." He added that if it proves true that the Rabat plotters were bent on killing other Arab leaders in addition to King Hussein, then [Abu Iyad] is guilty of "high treason."

```
3. Other comments volunteered by Salameh to
   EMBOFF included assertion that USG [U.S.
   government] could discount possibility of
   PFLP [Popular Front for the Liberation of
   Palestine] terror operations in New York or
   elsewhere during the next few weeks. He
   claimed that [George] Habash had been warned
   strongly against doing anything to besmirch
   PLO image while UNGA debate is in progress.
4. Comment: We suspect that much of Salameh's
   remarks RE: Abu Iyad were calculated for our
   benefit. At same time, there may be some truth
   in his contention that [Abu Iyad] has a lot to
   answer for when and if he returns to Beirut.³
```

I read and reread this incredible document during the spring of 2008. Ali Hassan Salameh, the Red Prince—the mastermind behind the Munich Massacre and countless other terrorist operations—had sat down with "EMBOFF" (CIA agents and probably a U.S. Embassy political officer; maybe the Regional Security Officer [RSO] as well) to discuss a rogue assassination plot hatched by Abu Iyad and his loyalists targeting King Hussein and other Arab notables during a key moment in PLO history. Some twenty Arab leaders had gathered at Rabat to discuss the Israeli-Palestinian situation, and for the first time the Arab nations recognized the legitimacy of the PLO's territorial claims.

At first, King Hussein vigorously opposed the Rabat Declaration. He signed it only after the other Arab nations essentially bribed him with an annual subsidy of $300 million.

Then, in early November 1974, Salameh sat down with U.S. intelligence agents to discuss the inner tensions and politics among the PLO, its rival factions, and its rival leaders. Salameh was given the code name MJTRUST/2 by the CIA. The TRUSTs were the code names for liaisons with PLO/Fatah security. TRUST/1 was PLO chairman Arafat, according to a former CIA clandestine services officer who worked the Palestinian account. No wonder Abu Iyad had been left behind when Arafat flew to New York.

Suddenly, some confusing details started to make sense. Salameh had traveled with his boss to the United States, something that could never have happened without State Department approval.[4] The U.S. government knew that Salameh had planned and ordered the Khartoum operation that killed our ambassador to Sudan. State had allowed a known terrorist whose actions had cost the lives of countless innocents to enter the country.

The CIA probably worked behind the scenes with the State Department to make it happen. Salameh was an asset, an informer. As a result, he received his visa and shadowed Arafat in New York.

In 2008, my media sources told me that they sat down with three senior-level, retired CIA agents to acquire deep background on Alon and his murder. All three independently confirmed that Salameh had been a CIA source. They also noted that the agency had two more Black September sources at the time, neither of whom they identified.

From Beirut, I received additional confirmation of the Red Prince's connection with the CIA. My contact in Lebanon had sat down with one of his sources, a man who had spent most of his life serving the PLO. This man discussed Salameh at length and asserted that the Israelis did not kill him in 1979 as an act of revenge for the Munich Massacre but rather because of his relationship with the CIA. Not only were Salameh's ties with the agency well known within the PLO; Arafat used them as a back-channel means of communicating with the U.S. government.

According to my sources, Salameh's relationship with the CIA began in Beirut in 1969, when CIA case officer Robert Ames first made contact with him.[5] Arafat blessed that meeting, as he made a point of keeping lines of communication open with every player in the Middle East who could help the PLO and its cause.[6]

Over the years, the CIA made direct overtures to the Red Prince to turn him into a double agent. The agency first offered him cash, which offended Salameh and caused to him break off communication for several years. The CIA had failed to understand that the Red Prince had plenty of money and was ideologically, not economically, motivated.

Ames refused to give up and reached out to the Red Prince again in the mid-1970s. This time the two men met face-to-face in Kuwait. Salameh had received Arafat's approval to do so. Although he never became a double agent, he did serve as an informant for the CIA at Arafat's behest and passed along information that the PLO chief personally approved. That said, much of what Salameh ultimately shared with his CIA handlers proved to be accurate.

Who was playing whom here? Did the CIA realize that Salameh was manipulating its agents, providing only what Arafat wanted the agency to know? The Red Prince played a dangerous game, walking the fine line between conduit and traitor. It was a role he embraced with cunning and skill.

In the mid-1970s, a parallel game was played out between two nations in the midst of forming a new military alliance. The Israelis had established an intelligence foothold in the United States and had used Joe Alon to expand it even as he functioned as the liaison between the Israeli and U.S. air forces. Simultaneously, the CIA had a back door into Israel's most deadly nongovernmental enemy: Black September. The shadowy world of intelligence and espionage operations exists in the gray areas of morality. It is a place where the ends justify the means and pragmatism almost always wins out over idealism and adherence to noble values. And in 1973, Joe Alon's murder threatened to reveal the depths of the mutual betrayals entangling the United States and Israel. Cooperation and full disclosure would unravel the deals made behind the scenes.

No wonder both sides simply let the matter drop. Everyone had too much to lose if the truth had come out. In the end, the game consumed almost all the players. By mid-1973, most of the leaders of Black September were dead. The Red Prince and his entourage burned to ashes in his Chevrolet on a Beirut street in 1979. Robert Ames died in 1983 when Imad Mugniyah and Hezbollah blew up the front half of the U.S. Embassy in Beirut. Abu Iyad was next to go in 1991. Mugniyah was killed by a car bomb in Damascus, Syria, on February 12, 2008. No one knows exactly who killed him, although Mossad is on the top of most suspect lists.

On the Israeli side, all the major players are gone as well. Golda Meir died of cancer in 1978. Mordechai Gur died in 1995. Zvi Zamir is one of the few who remains alive, an old warrior whose days with Mossad have long since passed into legend. Zamir also drafted the original orders for the Wrath of God Squads sanctioned by Golda Meir.

The Capitol Hill briefings contained one more lead that Ed and I could pursue. The professor who had provided the logistical support for the Alon assassination had evidently escaped prosecution. Ed and I data-mined our way through the FBI files we had and discovered the professor's identity.

As a boy of fourteen in 1948, the professor lived through the Israeli War of Independence while living in a small Palestinian village. In the violence that swept across the region that year, his aunt drowned herself rather than submit to a sexual assault by a group of Yemeni volunteers occupying the village during the fighting with Jewish forces.

In 1973, the professor was teaching at an American university. The FBI, suspecting him of a role in the plot to kill Golda Meir at JFK Airport, interviewed and released him.

In all likelihood, he was Black September's point man in the D.C. area. In Europe, they used outwardly pacifistic intellectuals as cell leaders in key cities or regions. The professor, a middle-aged academic, fit that bill.

He remained at the university for at least a few more months, publishing articles in professional journals. Later in the 1970s, he moved to Beirut. Subsequently, he relocated to a Middle Eastern country where he currently resides, protected by a state sponsor of terror. Efforts to interview the professor have failed.

CHAPTER SEVENTEEN

TRACKING THE KILLERS

2009

After all these years, Ed and I had finally managed to piece together most of the puzzle surrounding Joe Alon and his assassination. By the summer of 2009, there remained only a few unresolved questions:

- Who ordered the assassination?
- Who planned it?
- Who were the killers on Trent Street that night, and what was their fate?

A retired FBI agent who worked the MURDA investigation provided the first tangible lead on the killers' fate.

Stan learned from a colleague in the FBI Baltimore office that Mossad had tracked down Alon's murderers and tailed them to

Cyprus. The Israelis had blown up a yacht they were on off the Cypriot coast. Case closed. No further need to go any further with the investigation.[1] If true, we figured the case was closed by "exception," meaning the killers were eliminated by Mossad and would never be brought to justice in a U.S. court of law.

Not long after, the FBI dropped the case and destroyed the evidence. Mossad's information probably had not been enough for the FBI to close the case; some other, higher-level and informal contact must have taken place between the two agencies. That explained why the evidence had been destroyed. If the killers were dead, what was the point of hanging onto such material? If a foreign intelligence service tells you off-the-record that the suspects were eliminated, it is enough to place a memo in the file and move on. But we never found that memo and believed that some things were better off not being documented as part of the formal record.

Except that it was not actually resolved, and a year later, when Ali Hassan Salameh revealed the details of the assassination attempt to the CIA, there was no way to reopen the case. My working theory is Salameh was the source of the document disclosed to the Senate hearing. But there would never be an arrest, never be a time for the accused to stand before a judge and jury. With the evidence destroyed, the FBI would never be able to secure a conviction.

Ed and I tried to confirm the assassination on the yacht. Shortly after his encounter with the Mossad agent, Stan recalled seeing a news article in a Washington paper about a yacht blowing up off Cyprus.

We conducted a thorough search and found no such article in any major American papers. To the best of our knowledge, no yacht exploded in the eastern Mediterranean in the mid-1970s.[2]

We also reached out to our contacts, both inside and outside government service, to see if anyone had heard of such an Israeli hit. Nothing like it had ever come across anyone's radar. The story smelled like a total fabrication or disinformation, designed to get the FBI to quit investigating the case so that the Americans would not discover Joe's undercover role in the United States.

At the same time, Ed and I grew hopeful that we could still find the killers. Perhaps they had avoided the bloody fate of so many of their Black September comrades, and they were still alive.

———

In December 2007, my contact in Beirut wrote to my electronic dead drop. Inside the Drafts folder, I found a message that offered insight into Black September and some of its key players.

My contact had arranged a meeting with his source, who had served as a high-ranking member of the Palestine Liberation Organization in Lebanon during the 1970s. The two spent an afternoon together, discussing old times. The aging Palestinian offered considerable insight into Black September, starting with confirmation that it was not a stand-alone or monolithic organization with a central command. Rather, it was a name used to carry out violent attacks that the PLO leadership ordered and planned but did not want to be linked to in the court of world opinion. At the time, Chairman Arafat was trying to build the PLO into a respectable, legitimate representative body for the Palestinian people and could not allow it to be seen as an agent of terror. Yet after the Jordanian massacre in September 1970, which gave birth to Black September, Arafat faced a no-win situation. Rival and radicalized factions within the Palestinian political scene threatened his standing. If the PLO did not respond violently, it would have lost credibility with the Fedayeen foot soldiers and with the Palestinian people.

The Palestinian told my contact that both Mossad and the CIA wasted a lot of effort on an organization that had no central objective save sporadic, strategic acts of revenge. In his view, Abu Youssef had been the most important leader within the cadre that functioned as Black September's leadership. He was the one who planned the assassination of Wasfi al-Tell, the Jordanian prime minister, in Cairo. That was the first attack Black September took credit for, and it served as ample revenge for the 1970 massacre on the East Bank. The Palestinian source then went on to recount how Youssef died at the hands of Israeli commandos during Operation Spring of Youth in April 1973.

Then the conversation turned to Salameh. The old Palestinian lit up and spoke lovingly of the Red Prince. He claimed to have been something of a father figure for the young man after his biological one died in the fight against the Jews in 1948. He knew Salameh intimately. He also spoke candidly about him and was clearly disappointed with the path that he ultimately had chosen. In his opinion, Salameh was not a great planner or tactician. Nor was he an inspiring leader. He was too distracted, too obsessed with the high life. Ruefully, he spoke of Salameh's increasing drug use during the 1970s. Toward the end of the conversation, the Palestinian asserted that had the Israelis not assassinated him in 1979, the Red Prince probably would have ended up a homeless drug addict wandering the streets of Beirut.

Then my contact steered the conversation to Joe Alon and his assassination. The Palestinian remembered the event but not Joe's name. He simply called Joe "the Israeli diplomat." He did not know the names of the assassins dispatched to kill Joe, nor did he really care. He did state that Black September never could have carried out the operation without non-Palestinian support within the United States. He would not elaborate further on that point.

Non-Palestinian support? Perhaps the FBI was right to suspect the Black Panthers after all. The Cleaver faction of the Black Panther Party consistently surfaced in the FBI files linked to the case. In the FBI files, Ed and I found that early in the investigation, a group of Arab students at a university in Washington, D.C., had come under suspicion. In reality, that line of inquest seemed more logical than the Black Panthers. The FBI files also had information that Kuwaitis were somehow linked, but without any details.

The next message that arrived in the dead drop from my contact in Beirut was the one I had been waiting thirty-five years to read. My associate had met with an elderly former Black September member. He was one of the last alive, and his memories are perhaps the last link to what happened back in the 1970s.

Wizened, with missing teeth and dressed in an ill-fitting suit, the old operative had been on the periphery of the PLO's leadership core. He had known both Abu Iyad and Salameh quite well. He spoke proudly of his association with Abu Iyad, whom he still admired. One day, he told my contact, he had gone to Abu Iyad's office near Beirut Arab University. Abu Iyad was in a jubilant mood, and as soon as he greeted our source, he exclaimed, "We finally got the bastard! This will teach the Israelis an unforgettable lesson!"[3]

Abu Iyad was referring to what the source recalled was the assassination of an Israeli Mossad officer in the United States. He did not remember the victim's name, but my contact clearly could tell he was referring to Joe Alon. The operation had been in the works for months and was designed to retaliate for the Israeli Air Force bombing of Palestinian targets in Lebanon in the wake of the Munich Massacre. Abu Iyad had ordered the hit, and Salameh had planned it.

Our source vividly recalled walking in one day as Abu Iyad was talking on a telephone. He overheard much of the conversation and related it to my Beirut contact. That phone call from thirty-five years ago gave us the first solid lead on the killer's whereabouts. Abu Iyad was talking about securing an Algerian passport for the "hero" who had killed the Israeli Mossad agent in Washington, D.C. The Black September leader was trying to get him to a safe haven in Latin America. My working theory is that Salameh was on the other end of the call with Abu Iyad. Knowing how important the mission was, the Red Prince would have wanted to be the messenger. The two were probably talking in code, using cover names.

Unfortunately, the elderly Palestinian did not remember the name of the assassin. We discovered that name through another Palestinian source, who must remain unnamed to safeguard his identity. That information was confirmed by Ed from a terrorist released from U.S. custody (name redacted) shortly before he was deported and flown to an undisclosed location abroad.

———————

These two men confirmed the identity of the killer. The man who pulled the trigger on the night of Alon's assassination was a young Palestinian named Hassan Ali.[4] His family lived on the West Bank. In the 1960s, the family settled in Lebanon. As a boy, Ali loved horses and often was seen riding between the Sabra Palestinian refugee camp in Beirut and the Martyrs Cemetery.

As an adult, Ali joined the Fedayeen and fought the Jordanians during the September 1970 battles. After the Munich

Olympics massacre, he was recruited into Fatah-17, serving as one of the most loyal members within that elite intelligence and security force that protected Arafat and other PLO leaders. When Abu Iyad ordered Salameh to plan Joe Alon's assassination, he turned to his inner circle within Fatah-17 and selected Ali and one other man for the mission. Neither man had been involved in any terror operation before, so they were not known to western intelligence agencies and would not have had trouble entering the United States. They would be one-shot operatives. After accomplishing their mission, they would flee to South America and live under assumed names.[5]

According to my Beirut sources, Black September had learned of the party in Chevy Chase at least two weeks before the event. They had been tracking Alon, his movements, and his schedule very closely, which confirmed that all the suspicious events at the house on Trent Street were indeed part of a preoperational surveillance effort.

In the early-morning hours of July 1, 1973, Ali stepped out of the darkness and emptied his revolver into Joe Alon as he stood beside his Ford Galaxie. Ali's associate, whose name we never learned, drove the getaway car that Dvora saw moving down the street. The local support network, organized by a Middle Eastern professor, disposed of the car and helped get Ali and his associate out of the country. Ali traveled to Porto Alegre, Brazil, where he lived under an assumed name. Another source who had been close to Abu Iyad stated that Ali had received permanent residence status in Brazil under a pseudonym.[6]

After three decades, layers of deception, lies, false leads, and dead ends, Ed and I had finally found a suspect. Now one last thing remained: capturing him and bringing him to justice.

———————

I realized that this was probably an almost hopeless task, but I could not give up after we had come so far. Through 2008 and into 2009, I used all of the connections through my old-boys' network, Israeli back channels, and those that Strategic Forecasting possesses in Brazil and Latin America to try to locate Ali. I reached out to spooks and spies as well as personal contacts. Everyone came up empty at first, but we had no evidence if Ali was still alive or not.

The search went on for months. Ed went to Interpol and tried to track Ali down through that avenue. That proved to be another dead end. Although I had no reason to discount our sources, the thought crossed my mind that the sources could have been playing us or passing along disinformation to throw us off the hunt. One becomes paranoid in this business trying to figure out intentions and motives.

Finally, we caught a break. Israeli back-channel sources confirmed that the assassin was still alive, living in the Palestinian community of Porto Alegre, Brazil. We were closing in on him. Ed and I began to wonder what we would do if our back-channel sources did finally find him.

If we tipped the FBI, the State Department, or DSS, they could snatch him in Brazil and fly him to the States, where he could stand trial.[7] Such an operation would be tremendously risky. The more we probed, the more we suspected that Ali had some form of protection, the nature of which was not clear. Trying to get accurate ground truth became problematic. By this time, I had established Israeli back-channels who were also looking for the suspect in Brazil. Sending a team of agents to get Ali out of the country under such circumstances would be foolhardy; if detected, it could set off a diplomatic nightmare for the United States. Besides, because the evidence had been destroyed in the 1970s, there would be no way to secure a conviction in a federal or state court. Still, we continued the search for him, even as the question of what we might do should we find him dogged me.

In late 2009, we received a tip. Someone had warned Ali that somebody or some organization was actively searching for him. Without hesitating, he had bolted from his Brazilian hideout and flown to Lebanon. I think Ali knew we were on the hunt.

My contact in Beirut grew extremely nervous and became fearful of retribution by terrorists, specifically Hezbollah. After all, he had to live there, which I understood completely. I didn't want to place my source in harm's way by asking too many more questions. His Black September and PLO sources, fearful for their lives, clammed up. Everyone was now hyperalert and very security conscious. My contact discovered that Hezbollah had taken Ali in as a token of appreciation for what he had done in 1973 and was protecting him somewhere in the Bekaa Valley in Lebanon, again showing the value of the BSO operation against the Israelis and the importance of Joe. He had gone to ground again, using a new alias that I did not have access to, protected by the poster-child of terrorism: Hezbollah.

For me, he was out of reach. The long pursuit had come to an end, and my role in this three-decade-old drama had reached its final act. I could either walk away and forget the entire affair or make one final contact in the hope that it would give closure to all those involved. Joe's daughters needed that; I had vowed that I would bring justice to their father's killer. But what is justice in a world of gray? Certainly, Ali would never be tried in a U.S. court of law. Too much time had passed, we lacked eyewitnesses, and the evidence had been destroyed, eliminating any hope of DNA analysis. The Lebanese government would never help, and Hezbollah would never turn him over to anyone. I had been down this road with Hasan Izz-Al-Din. Few options were left.

I thought about Mossad. The suspect may have stopped looking over his shoulder, protected by a notorious terrorist organization with a long history of violence. From a psychological perspective, Ali's guard may be down as he is under the protective umbrella of Hezbollah, which roams Lebanon with impunity; he felt secure. For once, time might have been on our side. I had old contacts within the Israeli intelligence services left in Mossad's ranks with a sense of justice who might prove sympathetic to what I had been doing to solve this case.

In late 2009, I sat down at my computer and sent my Israeli intelligence service contact a long and detailed email. I explained everything Ed and I had uncovered since 2006. I went through the case history, describing who Colonel Joe Alon was and what he meant to the IAF. Then I revealed who killed him, why, and where I knew the man to be hiding.

I finished and reread the email. What would the Israelis do with this information? I wondered. If anyone could get to Ali even while under Hezbollah protection, it would be Mossad. A trial in Israel was not likely. There were only two likely scenarios here: Mossad could simply ignore the information. Colonel Alon had died so long ago, perhaps his murder no longer mattered. The intelligence game was different now; the days of the Wrath of God Squads and tit-for-tat murders had been relegated to the past. There were too many lawyers overseeing every aspect of the intelligence business today. Then again, the Israelis have a long

memory, and a second scenario might play out.[8] Perhaps they really had not been able to find Alon's killer in 1973. Black September was a formidable adversary and had covered its tracks well
during many of the operations it carried out after Munich.
Maybe, just maybe, the Israelis would do something about Alon's
murder now.

Long into the night, I thought about Joe Alon. His family had
been wiped out in the violence that claimed most of Europe's
Jews. He had fled his native Czechoslovakia for a fresh start in Israel, where he helped shape and form the IAF. He played a vital
role in the 1956 war and in preparing a whole new generation of
fighter pilots for 1967's Six-Day War and 1973's Yom Kippur
War. He had left an indelible mark on his nation, helping to secure its freedom from destruction at the hands of its numerous
Arab enemies.

At the end of his military career, he came to the United States
as a diplomatic representative.[9] In that role, he helped redefine
the nature of the military alliance between the United States and
Israel, an achievement that had had lasting consequences to the
United States and the entire Middle East for the next forty years.
He was a quiet hero to the State of Israel in a time period when
heroes were needed. Behind the scenes, he played another, darker
role. After the Munich Massacre, Mossad became fixated on Black
September. Joe was swept into that dynamic and almost certainly
had been running—or at least trying to cultivate—a network of
informants and turncoats. It was a game that had cost him his life.

His Black September connections turned the tables on him.
With help from either the Black Panthers or Arab students from
local D.C. universities, Joe was watched for months. Once Black
September established his true identity, patterns, and routines,
they realized they had a prime opportunity to deliver a stinging

blow to Israel. Assassinating a war hero within sight of the U.S. capital would have had a lasting effect on Mossad and the IAF.

When the preoperational surveillance was completed, Abu Iyad was given the green light to proceed. He ordered Salameh to plan the assassination, even as the loose network of Black September sympathizers in the D.C. area, including a university professor, stayed on their quarry's tail.

On July 1, 1973, it all came together for Abu Iyad and the Red Prince. Hassan Ali slipped from behind a tree in Joe's front yard and ended his life with a .38 caliber pistol. The murderer had escaped all reckoning for thirty-six years, although Mossad had effectively eliminated Ali Hassan Salameh, the tactical commander behind the operation.[10] Maybe Mossad felt that their job was done when Salameh had been killed in Beirut? Alon's shooter was a foot soldier, but in my eyes he was still a killer.

I recalled the phone conversations I had with Yola and Rachel, the pain of that night still evident in their voices. Their father's death had shadowed their lives; their mother had died without knowing the truth. Their perseverance had been unwavering; relentless with minimal help. Two nations should have done more. I should have done more.

That did it. I looked up at the computer screen, moved the mouse, and sent the email.

Long into the night, I sat and stared into the darkness and thought about what justice really means in a world perpetually on fire.

EPILOGUE

JUSTICE

February 2010

Almost thirty-seven years after Joe's death, the Sword of Gideon struck one final blow in a war that began at the Summer Olympics in Munich, in what was then West Germany. It is ironic that something so public should end so quietly.

The last of the Black September assassins has been hunted down.

One night, as I prepared to go to bed, my BlackBerry chimed as a message arrived. It was sitting atop the Bible on my nightstand, encased in the Otter Box protective shell I purchased for it when I first discovered this remarkable device. How the spies and spooks of the 1970s would have loved such a communication tool. Instead of a stylus and a Short Range Agent Communication (SRAC), the BlackBerry grants access to information and contacts across the globe in a way that would have been incomprehensible to those of Joe Alon's generation.

I reached for the phone. The chime signified an incoming text message, and I saw that it originated with my Mossad friend.

I read the words once, twice, a third time. I sat down on the edge of the bed and looked across at my desk. The lantern I had always used to read by still sat next to piles of documents and old photographs. My eyes passed over a black-and-white image of the Lebanese street in the aftermath of the Red Prince's assassination. Burned car, twisted metal. Mossad's work once again.

I looked at the sticky notes affixed to the wall in tidy rows that traced all the twists and turns in the Alon case. That desk and those notes represented decades of hard work and years of frustration; they marked my obsession.

Why had I been so consumed by this case? Was it for Joe? He was a man who served his nation at a pivotal time in its history, only to die on the battlefield of terror. For years I had told myself I was doing it for him. A man who gave his life for his country deserved better than what had happened in the wake of his death. Then I met his children and felt their pain with every email and phone conversation we shared. Their unresolved anguish propelled me forward, and I had sworn that I would do all within my power to bring them resolution.

But that still did not explain the years I had spent trying to solve this crime. For that, I had to turn inward and look inside my own heart. When I was sixteen years old, a man was brutally murdered in my quiet world. All my life I had known nothing but the safety of my community and the security of my parents' home and love. When I came downstairs and saw the headline that summer morning, something changed forever inside me. Violence had reached deep within the town I had known and claimed a schoolmate's father.

Joe's death had sent me in a search to reclaim that sense of safety, and my life became one devoted to protecting others. In the process, my narrow and naive worldview was shattered by the realities of hijackings, car bombings, murders, assassinations, and torture. In my years overseas and serving with the Diplomatic Security Service, I saw things average Americans would struggle to comprehend. I witnessed the low regard for human life common in many parts of the world. Over time, I came to realize that the violence that invaded my quiet suburban neighborhood in 1973 was not an aberration at all; the aberration was my community, my state, and my country. We were, and are, the last oasis in a world consumed by violence and human depravity. And for most of my adult life, I stood on the ramparts between the two.

I was not just solving Joe's murder. I was solving the riddle of my own life's path. The choices I made, the career I chose, and the way I governed myself all were influenced by that July day in 1973.

It was over now at last. I looked down at the text message again, a burst transmission of sorts from one side of the world to another between aging cold warriors. It did not say much. I would not have expected anything more. I did not want the details, anyway.

I held the BlackBerry in both hands. For a moment, images of old friends rushed before my eyes, men and women—agents and officers—who had died in the struggle to fight the world's raging flames. There are so many of them, killed in the line of duty at embassies around the world, or in the field somewhere, or here at home. We all have done our best to keep the wildfire from our shores, but the cost has been grievously high.

The older I get, the more often I find something that triggers old memories. The smell of Old Spice, a particular type of car passing me on an empty street, a Springsteen song on the radio, a firecracker exploding in the distance—all of these bring back the places and times that will always haunt me. I stepped into the fray, met cold-blooded killers face-to-face, and knew the nature of evil before I turned twenty-five. By the time I was forty, I had become intimately familiar with the worst of human nature. In every case, I saw the aftermath as well and watched helplessly as those who survived these random acts of terror struggled to piece together their lives and move forward. I always thought that by running down those who had harmed them and ensuring that they did not harm again, I could provide a little comfort to their victims.

The text message said, "The [Ali] matter has been resolved."

I rose from the bed and hit the delete button. Closure at last. It would never stop the pain—I realize that now—but at least the loop had been closed. It was time for all of us to move on. With my old yellow lab in tow, I stepped through the front door into the night. Tomorrow, a new chapter would begin.

ACKNOWLEDGMENTS

Sometimes in the counterterrorism business, and in life, your only decisions are bad ones. I made a bad one many years ago when I failed to solve this case while in an official capacity to do so. The murder of Colonel Joe Alon, a hero of the State of Israel, has haunted me for many, many years. It is hard to explain, but as I grow older and look back on the unsolved cases, the balls dropped and leads not followed, I am left with a tremendous amount of regret and guilt. To be blunt, I needed to solve this case for the many victims I could not or failed to help. Perhaps it is the fog of memories that haunt me as I think about a life of mistakes, bad decisions, voices of deceased family members lingering in my head, lost childhood friends, and darn good dogs that have passed away. It was time to let go.

No author writes a book without help, and I needed more than most. John Bruning Jr., a brilliant military historian, aviation expert, and good friend, helped make sense of how important Colonel Joe Alon was in the grand scheme of endless Israeli battles to save their nation and how his death impacted the Cold War. I have never known a man who knows more about aircraft and firefights in the sky. John provided clarity and content to a book badly in need of his talents. For that, I am grateful. I thank you, my friend.

I am indebted to Detective Ed Golian of the Montgomery County, Maryland, Police Department, Cold Case Squad, and FBI Special Agent Stan Orenstein (retired) in ways that I could never repay. These two men have been extraordinary. The case would not have been solved without their desire to do the right thing and to help a burned-out old agent like myself. Thank goodness for the old boy network.

Bethesda-Chevy Chase Rescue Squad Life Members Kenny Holden, Chief David Dwyer, George Geibel, and Chief Ned Sherburne moved heaven and earth to assist. The squad's volunteer service is legendary in the Washington, D.C., area, and I am grateful to have been a member since 1975. The Montgomery County, Maryland, Police Officers Association has also been a tremendous asset. I'm honored to have worn that badge for a brief period of time. Best job I ever had.

The Alon daughters have suffered more than any family should. I hope this book helps heal the pain of the loss of their father in some small way. I am also very, very sorry I did not do more when I was in an official capacity to do so. I take full responsibility for my inaction. I hope they will forgive me. Their father would have been very proud of their perseverance and quest for information.

Jim Hornfischer is a brilliant literary agent. He refused to give up on this story. I thank him. Alessandra Bastagli, my editor at Palgrave Macmillan, and her assistant, Colleen Lawrie, deserve a tremendous amount of credit for believing in me and Joe's story. I would also like to thank Erica Warren at Palgrave for her tireless efforts.

But more importantly, I am blessed to work every day around the highest-quality minds and brilliant analysts at Strategic Forecasting, under the visionary direction of Dr. George Friedman and his wife, Meredith. Don Kuykendall, Stratfor's president and chairman of the board, has been unwavering in his ongoing support. Stratfor's Tactical Team, led by my good friend and former Diplomatic Security Service counterterrorism Special Agent Scott "Stick" Stewart, with Anya Alfano and Korena Zucha, has been highly supportive. You will not find better analysts in the intelligence arena than those we have at Stratfor. Brian Genchur, Stratfor's media expert, has also provided tremendous assistance.

Jose and Monica Flores, exemplars of the American Dream, kept me going.

Adam Goldman and Randy Herschaft of the Associated Press deserve a very special thanks. I would not want either of them hunting me. Their quest for Joe's killers has been relentless.

The old boy network of current and former special agents, cops, journalists, and spooks (many of whom do not want any credit) has provided tremendous assistance in this thirty-year case.

I would like to thank my children, Jimmy, Katie, and Maddie, for their unwavering love and support. As I said in my book *Ghost*, follow your dreams and make a difference in the world.

Finally, to my wife, Sharon, I truly am blessed to have had you with me through the journey of life. Without your love and support, I would not have made it. God must have a special place in heaven for people like you.

Fred Burton
Austin, Texas

TIMELINE

1929	Joseph Placzek (a.k.a. Yosef [Joe] Alon) is born at Ein Harod in Israel.
1931	Placzek's parents are forced to return to Czechoslovakia.
1939	Placzek is sent to England to escape the Nazis.
1942	Ali Hassan Salameh (a.k.a. Abu Hassan), the son of Hassan Salameh, is born.
1948	Placzek changes his name to Joseph Alon; he emigrates to Israel and joins the Israeli Air Force's (IAF) first pilot's training course.
1953	Alon becomes one of Israel's first jet pilots.
Jan. 4, 1954	Alon marries his wife, Dvora.
1955	Alon is appointed to fly the Ouragan bomber and would later fly Mirage fighters.
Oct. 20, 1955	The Sinai Campaign begins.
1967	Alon is an IAF commander in the Six-Day War, and Salameh is appointed by Arafat as commander of his personal guard, called Force 17.
1969	CIA case officer Robert C. Ames makes first contact with Salameh, whose CIA code name is MJTRUST/2.

1970	Alon is appointed military air attaché to the Israeli embassy in Washington, D.C.
Sept. 6, 1970	The Popular Front for the Liberation of Palestine (PFLP) attacks and hijacks four airplanes from various European cities.
1971	The Black September Organization (BSO) is created by Yasser Arafat. Salameh is appointed as chief of operations.
Mar. 15, 1971	Salameh coordinates the explosion of a 16,000-ton oil tank in Rotterdam, the Netherlands, on behalf of the BSO.
Nov. 27, 1971	The BSO kills Wasfi al-Tell, the Jordanian prime minister, in the Cairo Sheraton in Egypt.
Dec. 15, 1971	Salameh coordinates the ambush of Ziad Al-Rifa'i, the Jordanian ambassador in London.
May 9, 1972	Belgian Sabena flight 571, en route from Brussels to Tel Aviv via Vienna, is hijacked by four BSO operatives.
Aug. 4, 1972	Salameh coordinates the blowing up of oil storage tanks in Trieste, Italy, burning 200,000 gallons of oil.
Sept. 5, 1972	The BSO carries out an attack at the Munich Olympics. A massacre ensues.
Sept. 13, 1972	Israeli prime minister Golda Meir authorizes Mossad to hunt down and eliminate those responsible for the Munich Massacre.
Sept. 8, 1972	Mossad assassinates Mahmoud Hamshari, the PLO's unofficial representative in Paris, France.
Sept. 10, 1972	Mossad case officer Zadok Ophir is assassinated by the BSO in Brussels, Belgium.
Sept. 17, 1972	The BSO mails sixty-four letter bombs from Amsterdam to various Israeli diplomats around the world.
Oct. 16, 1972	Mossad assassinates BSO operative Wael Zu'aytir, Arafat's second cousin, in Rome.

Dec. 28, 1972   Salameh dispatches four BSO operatives to Bangkok, Thailand, to attack the Israeli embassy there. Facility seizure is unsuccessful.

Feb. 21, 1973   An Israeli fighter aircraft shoots down a Libyan Arab Airlines jet in the Sinai, killing one hundred.

Mar. 1, 1973   The BSO attacks the Saudi embassy in Khartoum, killing U.S. ambassador Cleo Noel and U.S. deputy chief of mission George Moore.

Apr. 6, 1973   In Paris, Mossad assassinates Dr. Basil Al-Kubaisi, a senior member of George Habash's PFLP and one of the planners of the attack at Lod Airport in 1972.

Apr. 9, 1973   Mossad places an improvised explosive device (IED) under the bed of Ziad Mokhsi, the PLO representative in Cyprus, killing him.

Apr. 9, 1973   Operation Spring of Youth begins in Lebanon.

June 28, 1973   Mohammed Boudia is assassinated by Mossad in Paris. The BSO allegedly replaces Boudia with Carlos the Jackal.

July 1, 1973   Joseph Alon is assassinated in Chevy Chase, Maryland. The *Voice of Palestine* radio broadcast claims credit for the assassination in retaliation for the murder of Mohammed Boudia.

July 21, 1973   In Lillehammer, Mossad kills an innocent Palestinian waiter, Ahmed Boushiki, who they believe is Ali Hassan Salameh, now known as "The Red Prince." Six Mossad operatives are arrested by the Norwegian authorities.

Oct. 6, 1973   Jewish Day of Atonement; the Yom Kippur War begins when Syrian and Egyptian armies coordinate a surprise invasion of the Golan Heights and the Sinai.

Dec. 1973   The BSO is dissolved by Arafat.

Nov. 13, 1973   Arafat and Salameh travel to New York City for the General Assembly meetings at the United Nations.

Apr. 19, 1974   *Al-Hawades* magazine reports that Ahmed Jabril took credit for the Alon killing.

Aug. 1975   The author joins the Bethesda-Chevy Chase Rescue Squad.

Feb. 3, 1976   All of the leads in the Alon killing are exhausted by the FBI, and the FBI administratively closes the case.

May 1977   Israeli prime minister Menachem Begin reissues the 1973 Golda Meir authorization for Mossad assassinations; they now include Salameh.

June 8, 1977   Salameh marries a former Miss Universe, Georgina Rizak, a Lebanese Christian.

Mar. 30, 1978   Dr. Wadi Haddad dies of poisoning. Mossad is suspected of killing Haddad, who was the first to hijack an El Al plane on July 28, 1968, and was one of the original founders of the PFLP.

Jan. 22, 1979   Salameh is assassinated by Mossad on Rue Verdun, Beirut, Lebanon.

May 14, 1979   The Red Prince's son is born.

Mar. 1982   The author becomes a police officer with the Montgomery County, Maryland, Police Department, assigned to the Wheaton District.

Nov. 1985   The author becomes a State Department special agent assigned to the Counterterrorism Division, along with Agent John Mullen, working for Division Chief Steve Gleason.

1986   The author formally reopens the Alon case within the Counterterrorism Division with Steve Gleason's authorization.

Jan. 14, 1991   Salah Khalaf (a.k.a. Abu Iyad) is killed along with Fatah security chief Abu al-Hawl.

June 8, 1992   PLO agent Atef Bseio is assassinated by Mossad's Caesarea unit in Paris.

Sept. 13, 1993	Yitzhak Rabin, President Bill Clinton, and Yasser Arafat sign the Oslo Accords.
1995	The author sends messages to the U.S. Embassy in Tel Aviv regarding the Alon case. These include a memorandum requesting that an update be sent to the Embassy of Israel. The messages go unanswered.
Nov. 4, 1995	Yitzhak Rabin is assassinated.
Jan. 1996	Israeli Shin Bet agents assassinate Hamas bomber Yihya "The Engineer" Ayash using a cell-phone IED.
Nov. 11, 2004	PLO chairman Yasser Arafat dies.
June 2006	The author's new quest for the killer of Joe Alon begins.
June 9, 2006	Stan Orenstein, the original FBI case agent, is interviewed concerning the Alon case.
June 28, 2006	The author has his first meeting with Detective Ed Golian at the Montgomery County Police Department Cold Case Squad to review the case and the outstanding leads.
Mar. 19, 2007	The author reinterviews now-retired FBI agent Orenstein and learns that the CIA was a huge obstacle. Shin Bet and Mossad were not cooperative.
Mar. 22, 2007	The author establishes contact with the Alon daughters. Rachel Alon provides the government of Israel's official response to the Alon murder.
Apr. 12, 2007	The author uncovers that in an interview with a Kuwaiti newspaper *Al Qabas* in February 1974, PFLP leader Ahmed Jabril claims that his organization was responsible for the Alon murder.
Apr. 20, 2007	A newly declassified CIA document from a 1978 CIA briefing to Capitol Hill of the BSO involvement in the assassination is provided by Associated Press (AP) investigative reporters Adam Goldman and Randy Herschaft, who were working on a story surrounding the anniversary of Alon's death.

Apr. 23, 2007   The author learns from Detective Golian that two nights
                 before the Alon shooting, two neighbors observed a light-
                 colored car with four or five males cruising the streets in
                 Somerset (Trent Street). The author also learns that on
                 the night of the murder, another neighbor observed a
                 light-colored car with rental tags, with four or five dark-
                 complexioned males, on Trent Street at 6:30 P.M. driving
                 slowly.

Apr. 25, 2007   The author discovers that Major General Mordechai
                 Gur, an Israeli military attaché at the Embassy of Israel,
                 was stationed at the Israeli embassy when Alon was
                 murdered.

June 27, 2007   Ashraf Marwan, one of Israel's most famous spies, dies a
                 mysterious death in London. Marwan played a crucial role
                 in the lead-up to the 1973 Yom Kippur War.

July 3, 2007   Detective Golian uncovers in the FBI files a message from
                 FBI Baltimore to FBI Washington Metropolitan Field
                 Office about the alleged surveillance of Alon by a group of
                 Georgetown University students.

May 21, 2007   Adam Goldman and Randy Herschaft of the AP provide
                 the author with a declassified CIA Capitol Hill briefing
                 document that reveals that the BSO was responsible for
                 Alon's murder.

Sept. 29, 2007   Detective Golian advises that his file reviews reveal a
                 suspect. "Hassan Ali" was one of two men assigned to kill
                 the Israeli ambassador to Washington, D.C.

Nov. 5, 2007   A confidential source in Beirut provides further
                 information on the suspect to the author.

Nov. 30, 2007   The Beirut source identifies an "old aide" to Abu Iyad,
                 which becomes a key find. Most of the BSO operatives
                 have been killed or have died.

Dec. 6, 2007   The author discovers that, according to Detective Golian,
                 while on the scene of the murder, one of the senior
                 Montgomery County police investigators was advised by
                 General Mordechai Gur that Alon was a spy working for

Mossad under the cover of a military attaché assigned to the Israeli embassy.

Jan. 2, 2008   The author discovers that, according to a confidential informant linked to the BSO, Abu Iyad played a crucial role in Alon's assassination. Abu Iyad used pro-Palestinian Arabs living in the United States in order to execute the plan. The source confirmed the involvement of Ali Hassan Salameh and Hassan Ali.

Jan. 25, 2008   The Beirut source advises that details of the Alon killing were in all probability stored in Abu Iyad's classified safe.

Jan. 27, 2008   The Beirut source advises that the last thing he knew about Ali dates back to 1975. By that time, Ali was in Brazil, in the state of Rio Grande du Sul, most likely in Porto Alegre.

Jan. 27, 2008   Interpol leads are sent to Brazil by the cold case detective.

Mar. 3, 2009   The investigation indicates that sketchy FBI intelligence surfaced in June 1973 about a hit team heading down to Washington, D.C., to carry out a hit on the Israeli ambassador.

Mar. 13, 2009   The author interviews a former Palestinian bodyguard and relative of Abu Iyad.

Mar. 26, 2009   Unidentified latent fingerprints are recovered on the 1960 Chevrolet parked inside the Alon garage, and the author discusses running traces through Interpol. The prints are the only physical evidence still in the possession of the local police.

Oct. 12, 2009   Detective Golian uncovers that the later-deported terrorist's mission in Conus was also to look at Israeli targets in Washington, D.C., and that the terrorist suspected that Ali was involved in the attack on Alon.

Dec. 18, 2009   The author establishes a back-channel dialogue with a trusted source inside the Israeli intelligence services.

Jan. 12, 2009   Latent fingerprint traces of the prints recovered from the crime scene are resubmitted for traces with the Israeli authorities. At the time of this writing, the Israelis have not responded to the request.

Jan. 10, 2010   The author conducts a video conference with the Alon daughters to discuss their mother's 1974 visit to the United States to discuss the murder.

Feb. 2010   Notification from the author's trusted source with the Israeli intelligence service indicates that "the [Ali] matter has been resolved."

NOTES

PROLOGUE

1. LaBarbara Bowman and Philip A. McCombs, "5 Shots Kill Israeli Aide in Bethesda," *Washington Post*, July 2, 1973.
2. I describe that life in an earlier book: Fred Burton, *Ghost: Confessions of a Counterterrorism Agent* (New York: Random House, 2008).
3. Montgomery County, Maryland, Police Department, master case number B327046. The original police file is contained in the Cold Case Squad, Montgomery County Police Headquarters.
4. FBI file number 185–118, code-named MURDA. The size of the original FBI file is unknown. The author obtained numerous documents through the Freedom of Information Act (FOIA); however, it is believed there are other classified files at both FBI Headquarters and FBI New York that have not been accessed. The bulk of the FBI files are heavily redacted.

CHAPTER 1

1. Although my father's Chevron gas station has been replaced by another brand, the physical layout of the gas station remains the same today as it did in 1973.
2. Montgomery County, Maryland, Police report of investigation, case number B327046. June 2006 interviews of the Montgomery County, Maryland, police officers at the scene: Tom Lowther, Robert McKenna, Jack Toomey, Ric Nelson, and William McKee.
3. June 2006 interviews of the first responders at the scene: Chief David Dwyer and Life Member Kenny Holden, Bethesda-Chevy Chase Rescue Squad, Bethesda, Maryland. The rescue squad was the first on the scene of the shooting. B-CC Rescue 17 and medic ambulance were staffed with Holden, Chief Dwyer, Dickie Mullens, Mark Knowles, Tom Rude, and Stan Parnes. Rescue 17 is visible in the background of the crime scene pictures. The author attempted to locate the original written report of the rescue call, but it has been lost or destroyed. Upon returning to the rescue

squad after the call, the crew would have written a report on a manual typewriter and placed it in a binder in the dispatch office. I was hopeful that it would contain information not in the police or FBI files.

4. LaBarbara Bowman and Philip A. McCombs, "5 Shots Kill Israeli Aide in Bethesda," *Washington Post*, July 2, 1973.

5. March 26, 2007, interview with Rachel and Yola Alon.

CHAPTER 2

1. The house today looks exactly like it did on the night of the murder. One of the original neighbors is still there and lives across the street from where the murder occurred. When the Alon daughters returned to Bethesda in June 2010, the neighbor welcomed the daughters into her home to spend the night.

2. July 12, 1973, teletype from FBI Los Angeles to FBI director discussing Alon's past in Czechoslovakia.

CHAPTER 3

1. B-CC Rescue Squad Life Member Dickie Mullens drove the victim to the hospital.

2. Dr. Janos Bacsanyi told Detective Ed Golian that his initial impressions were that Colonel Alon was shot with a submachine gun. Dr. Bacsanyi also said he dreaded telling Mrs. Alon that Colonel Alon was dead and recalled Mrs. Alon saying that the attack was done by terrorists. Montgomery County Police Department supplemental report in case file; Detective Ed Golian, interview with the author.

3. On March 3, 2009, FBI Special Agent Stan Orenstein (retired) told the author that General Gur stated Colonel Alon had nothing to do with intelligence at the scene of the murder. Gur stated Colonel Alon was not a member of Mossad (the Israeli intelligence agency, similar to the CIA).

4. In 1982, as a police officer with the MCPD, I first encountered FBI Special Agent Stan Orenstein at the scene of a bank robbery in Wheaton, Maryland. At the time, I had no idea he also had worked on the Alon case. The FBI's Resident Agency (remote office known as an RA that reported to Baltimore) was located on Georgia Avenue in Wheaton, Maryland, across from the Gate-of-Heaven Cemetery, where my good friend Sergeant Fred Davis of the U.S. Park Police is buried.

5. June 4, 2006, interview with FBI Special Agent Stan Orenstein (retired).

6. A navy veteran who had served in Saigon as a medical officer, Dr. Kornblum had an outstanding reputation for groundbreaking research into choking deaths and sudden infant death syndrome. Examining a fallen Israeli air hero was the first of a long list of autopsies Dr. Kornblum carried out on famous individuals. Later in his career, he became the Los Angeles

County Coroner and carried out autopsies on such notables as John Belushi, Natalie Wood, Karen Carpenter, Truman Capote, and William Holden.

7. "One shot through the heart inflicted fatal damage," according to the medical examiner in the official autopsy report.

8. Dr. Kornblum, deputy chief medical examiner, State of Maryland, conducted the autopsy, according to an FBI letterhead memorandum to the attorney general dated July 2, 1973.

9. There are numerous FBI teletypes in the master case file on the search for rental cars in an effort to develop leads. The suspect vehicle has never been found. Nor has the gun used to kill Colonel Alon ever been located.

CHAPTER 4

1. Bill Richards and Harold J. Logan, "Arab Sympathizers Investigated," *Washington Post*, July 3, 1973.

2. From News Dispatches, "Vows to Liquidate Terrorists," *Washington Post*, July 3, 1973.

3. March 26, 2007, interview of Rachel and Yola Alon. Since March 2007, the author has had several conversations with the daughters by telephone, email, and Skype. On June 8, 2010, the daughters (Rachel and Yola), Fred Burton, Detective Ed Golian, and Special Agent Stan Orenstein met at the Trent Street crime scene in an emotional reunion to discuss the case, along with a news crew from Israeli TV. Later that day, the daughters, Ed Golian, and Fred Burton met in the Cold Case Division of the Montgomery County Police Department to discuss the investigation.

4. While I was in the DSS, we used the term "Dark World" to describe the shadowy espionage and counterterrorism business.

CHAPTER 5

1. Details of the massacre can be found in Simon Reeve, *One Day in September: The Full Story of the 1972 Munich Olympics Massacre and the Israeli Revenge Operation "Wrath of God"* (New York: Arcade, 2000).

2. Yola Alon interviews with the author, April 25 and 26, 2007.

3. Rachel and Yola Alon, interviews with the author.

4. March 26, 2007, interview with Rachel and Yola Alon. The author attempted to contact Ephraim Halevy in June 2010; however, Halevy never responded. Halevy does not discuss the Alon killing in his 2006 memoir, *Man in the Shadows*, published by St. Martin's Press, but does disclose very interesting conversations and an exchange of letters with legendary CIA spymaster James Jesus Angleton. Specifically, Angleton encourages Halevy to explore the Soviet KGB relationship with PLO chairman Yasser Arafat, based on a surveillance photograph the CIA obtained in Moscow. In the

picture, Arafat is seen with a "bald man" known to the CIA as a KGB operative. Angleton encourages Halevy and Mossad to discover if Arafat
knew German because the KGB operative had been known to operate in
Karlshorst. Angleton subsequently learned that Arafat had studied engineering in Munich and knew German. Discussions in the book make clear
that Halevy and Angleton had a close personal relationship, with Halevy
visiting Angleton at his home prior to the latter's death. Interestingly, Angleton also maintained the CIA liaison account (a formal intelligence relationship established between governments) with Mossad while running
the CIA's operations against the Soviets. I cannot imagine a more powerful man in the intelligence business at the time with responsibility for both
Mossad and the KGB accounts during the height of the Cold War.
5. Rachel and Yola Alon, interviews with the author.
6. The family has several photographs of Joe Alon and Moshe Dayan together
   at various military events. See the photograph section for an example.
7. Dan Raviv and Yossi Melman, *Every Spy a Prince: The Complete History of
   Israel's Intelligence Community* (Boston: Houghton Mifflin, 1990). The book
   provides a fascinating insight into the history of Israel's intelligence community. Over the years, Melman has also been extremely helpful in an-
   swering obscure questions about Shin Bet (Israel's internal security service,
   similar to the FBI) and Mossad. I can think of no better go-to investigative journalist on Israeli intelligence operations.
8. In the FBI's MURDA file, Dr. Henry Kissinger, U.S. secretary of state,
   was provided with FBI letterhead updates (one-copy only or eyes only for
   the recipient) on the status of the investigation. Based on my personal
   knowledge of terrorism investigations, I do not find that unusual. The case
   would have been of extreme interest to the State Department due to the
   foreign policy ramifications and our diplomatic relations with Israel. In
   2008, Dr. George Friedman, Stratfor's founder and chief executive, asked
   Dr. Kissinger about the case on my behalf. However, Dr. Kissinger could
   not recall the details of the case.

CHAPTER 6

1. For details on the air war over North Vietnam, see Marshall L. Michel
   III's seminal work, *Clashes: Air Combat over North Vietnam, 1965–72* (An-
   napolis, MD: Naval Institute Press, 1997).
2. For details on the U.S. air effort over Korea, see *Korean War Aces* by Robert
   Dorr, Jon Lake, and Warren Thompson (United Kingdom: Osprey Publishing, 1995). See also John Bruning, *Crimson Sky: The Air Battle for Korea,
   1950–53* (Dulles, VA: Brassey's, 1999).
3. SEACAAL report. The report was published in May 1966. A follow up
   report reached the USAF's Pacific headquarters in December of 1966. Essentially, the lack of air-combat-maneuver training, combined with the

vastly different performance capabilities of USAF aircraft compared to their Soviet-built adversaries, created a perfect storm in which the USAF would suffer heavy losses. The reports forecasted this, but the USAF took no serious action as a result of them. The forward-deployed units ended up paying the price.

4. For more information on the Red Baron Reports, see Steve Davies, *Red Eagles: America's Secret MiG's* (New York: Osprey Publishing, 2008), pp. 24–26.

5. *USAF Fighter Weapons Review*, Fall 1989, p. 43.

6. Rolling Thunder began in mid-1965 and lasted until November 1968. It was this campaign that saw the USAF most heavily engaged during the Vietnam War.

CHAPTER 8

1. Dr. Ahron Bregman's book, *Israel's Wars: A History since 1947* (New York: Routledge, 2000), is a brilliant study on the history of the 1973 Yom Kippur War. Dr. Bregman was also the last person to talk to Ashraf Marwan, one of the most important Mossad spies (code-named "the Angel") who played an important role in the run-up to the Yom Kippur War. Marwan was the son-in-law of Egypt's President Nasser and was an Egyptian intelligence officer. On June 27, 2007, he died mysteriously in London, where he either was pushed or jumped from his balcony. After Marwan's death, the Egyptians gave him a hero's burial. As of July 2010, there is a coroner's inquest under way in the United Kingdom to determine the facts of his death. Marwan was writing a memoir about his life as a spy at the time when he passed away; however, the manuscript has not been found. His family believes Mossad killed Marwan and took the book. In the course of our research, we could find no direct links between Colonel Alon and Marwan, but we do know that Alon did make a visit to London in May 1973. We do not know why he went there, nor do we have any evidence of Alon meeting Marwan. Regardless, it is reasonable to assume that Alon would have had access to Marwan's intelligence in his role as air attaché in Washington. The author has had numerous conversations and email exchanges with Dr. Bregman discussing Marwan. It would have been fascinating to ask Marwan if he knew Colonel Alon. Unfortunately, we will never know the answer to that question.

CHAPTER 9

1. On June 4, 2006, Detective Ed Golian, Cold Case Squad, Montgomery County Police Department, and the author first spoke about the case. Since 2006, Ed and I have met on several occasions at the scene of the crime and driven the streets together rehashing the crime and the killer's

possible escape routes. We have also met at MCPD headquarters and the Bethesda District of the Montgomery County Police and exchanged countless telephone calls and emails surrounding the case.

2. Since June 2006, FBI Special Agent Stan Orenstein (retired) and I have exchanged numerous emails and discussed the investigation over the telephone. We have also met at the scene of the crime to discuss the murder.

CHAPTER 10

1. During this time period, the Russian KGB was training many radical terrorist groups, including Black September. Through the years, I've looked for a KGB nexus to the case, but have not found one.

2. We were unable to identify the identity of the Czech colonel; however, the persistence is a classic Eastern Bloc recruitment technique, as is using Alon's heritage as leverage. The fact that Joe reported the contact shows his loyalty to the State of Israel.

3. In looking at the FOIA FBI files, it appeared to me that the FBI may have had an operational asset or human source inside the Black Panther Party in Los Angeles. A good number of the FBI reports on the Black Panther Party originate from the Los Angeles Division of the FBI.

4. From the beginning of the FBI investigation, a persistent theme surfaced inside the MURDA case file with a working FBI theory that the Eldridge Cleaver faction of the Black Panther Party was involved in the murder.

5. Several interviews with Kenny Holden, life member of the B-CC Rescue Squad. Neither the police nor FBI files are clear as to whether or not there was any follow up on the lead.

6. Kathleen Cleaver, email exchange with the author, October 30, 2009, and November 1, 2009.

7. According to an FBI investigative update memorandum dated July 2, 1973, written by F. S. Putnam to Mr. E. S. Miller, the Department of State advised on July 1, 1973, that the broadcasts of Radio Cairo were monitored. According to the State Department, the Voice of Palestine announced, "Brothers, here is a news report on the death of the Zionist Deputy Military Attaché for the Air Affairs at the Zionist enemy's embassy in Washington. Three days after the assassination of the martyr Muhammad Bu Diyyah at the hands of the Zionist intelligence elements in Paris, Colonel Yosef Alon, the Air Attaché and Deputy Military Attaché of the enemy's embassy in Washington, was executed. This is the first execution operation carried out against a Zionist official in the United States."

8. "Vows to 'Liquidate Terrorists,'" *Washington Post,* July 3, 1973, p. A1; Bill Richards and Harold J. Logan, "Arab Sympathizers Investigated," *Washington Post,* July 3, 1973, p. A1.

CHAPTER 12

1. Interview in May 2008 with David Ignatius, author of *Agents of Innocence* (New York: W. W. Norton, 1987), a true-to-life fictional account of Ali Hassan Salameh and a noted authority on Salameh. Numerous books about Salameh (who was also known as Abu Hassan) discuss the Black September Organization; they include Aaron J. Klein, *Striking Back* (New York: Random House, 2005); Dan Raviv and Yossi Melman, *Every Spy a Prince* (Boston: Houghton Mifflin, 1990); and Simon Reeve, *One Day in September* (New York: Arcade, 2000). All are excellent reads for those interested in more information on Salameh or Black September. In the course of my research, I attempted to talk to Salameh's former wife, Georgina Rizak, in Cairo, to no avail.

2. Klein, *Striking Back*.

3. Simon Reeve, *One Day in September* (New York: Arcade, 2000), pp. 20–21.

4. Numerous books and my own knowledge of the organization indicated that Black September had several operational cells in many European cities. After the Munich Massacre, Mossad targeted many Palestinian operatives in Stockholm, Bonn, Cyprus, Copenhagen, Lillehammer, and Paris. An excellent read from the Palestinian perspective was written by Abu Iyad with Eric Rouleau, *My Home, My Land: A Narrative of the Palestinian Struggle* (New York: Times Books, 1978). Abu Iyad was also known as Salah Khalaf and was the leader of Black September. The book provides a wonderful look into Abu Iyad's mind-set and logic behind attacking Israeli targets.

CHAPTER 13

1. Aaron Klein, *Striking Back* (New York: Random House, 2005).

2. The Munich Massacre changed the way athletes are protected at international events. Today, the State Department's Diplomatic Security Service helps foreign liaison and security services with event management and protection. At the 1996 Olympics in Atlanta, where I had protective responsibility for the athletes, the Israelis insisted on extraordinary security, which created headaches for everyone. We had to give Shin Bet their own dorm, agree to large numbers of their protection agents being armed, and allow for enhanced and special security arrangements. In discussions with the Israelis in Atlanta, Shin Bet kept bringing up Munich. We were concerned about treating the Israeli athletes differently, which would cause their profile to be raised and elevate the threat. We much preferred for the Israeli athletes to blend in and keep a low profile. Needless to say, we lost that battle and were directed by Washington to give the Israelis everything they wanted. Munich looms large at every international event.

3. Michael Bar-Zohar and Eitan Haber, *Massacre in Munich* (New York: Routledge, 2010), p. 132.

4. Aaron J. Klein, *Striking Back: The 1972 Munich Olympics Massacre and Israel's Deadly Response* (New York: Random House, 2005).

CHAPTER 14

1. Aaron J. Klein's book *Striking Back: The 1972 Munich Olympics Massacre and Israel's Deadly Response* (New York: Random House, 2005) chronicles in great detail Mossad's assassination tactics and modus operandi.
2. Arafat was protected by the New York Police Department on his visit to the United Nations, and the department never responded to my request for information surrounding the trip. In reviewing the State Department cable traffic between Beirut and Washington on the visit, I learned that Ali Hassan Salameh was the U.S. Embassy point of contact on logistics surrounding the trip, negotiating on the number of bodyguards and weapons to be carried.
3. Rizak is married to a famous Egyptian singer now and lives in Cairo. The author attempted to contact Rizak to discuss Salameh, but my notes and a request for an interview were never answered.
4. Abu Iyad with Eric Rouleau, *My Home, My Land: A Narrative of the Palestinian Struggle*, trans. Linda Butler Koseoglu (New York: Times Books, 1981). This book is an interesting read and provides a unique window in my assessment for the motive for attacking Joe. On page 104, Abu Iyad discusses the "random bombings of Palestinian-populated areas and refugee camps, the indiscriminate killing of hundreds, indeed thousands of innocent civilians including children, women and old people . . . these assassinations [reference to BSO attacks] are far less shocking than the massacres organized by the Israeli army." Revenge can be a powerful motivator.
5. Interview with Yola Alon on April 27, 2008.
6. Confidential source of the author, former CIA Clandestine Services officer.
7. One week after Yola discovered the device, her father traveled to Canada. It is possible that Alon delivered the device to someone in Canada, because Yola never saw it again.
8. The Alon daughters knew the visitor as "Bob." He was a small, chubby man who appeared to be American. Ed Golian and I have attempted to identify Bob to no avail. To be blunt, there is not much to go on. If Bob was an intelligence officer, the visits to the Alon home make sense for privacy purposes and could mean that Alon did not want the Israeli embassy to know about them. It is also feasible that Bob was one of Alon's sources.

CHAPTER 15

1. Detective [x], Montgomery County Police Department, wrote the original supplemental concerning General Gur's comments that Alon was

Mossad. Gur told [x] that Alon was a spy working for Mossad under the cover of a military attaché.

2. General Gur's comments would clearly qualify as "an excited utterance" and usable in a court of law. Victims at the scene of the crime often make statements that typically are true due to the stress, chaos, and excitement of the events.

3. I strongly believe (and so does Detective Ed Golian) that Khalid Dunham Al-Jawary had a part to play in Colonel Alon's death. It is feasible that Al-Jawary was part of the U.S. planning or surveillance operations of Alon. Al-Jawary was recently released by the U.S. government after spending many years in jail for the March 4, 1973, attempted car bombing of Israeli prime minister Meir in New York City. Subsequent to Al-Jawary's release, Adam Goldman and Randy Herschaft of the Associated Press linked him to a bombing of an aircraft. In 1991, Al-Jawary was arrested in Rome as he flew to Abu Iyad's funeral. The link to Abu Iyad coupled with the targeting of the Israeli targets in New York City led me to believe that Al-Jawary had more to do with the killing of Alon than we may ever know. There are no coincidences in the Dark World of counterterrorism, only shades of gray. The FBI subsequently let Al-Jawary depart the country. It is rumored that he is back in the West Bank.

CHAPTER 16

1. August 4, 1978, CIA Memorandum for Michael Glennon and John Ritch, on the Staff of the Senate Foreign Relations Committee, OLC: 78–2965, bullet point #4. According to the memo, the two staffers visited CIA headquarters for a series of briefings related to requests for information by the Subcommittee of International Operations. A fair amount of the memorandum has been redacted by the U.S. government; however, the portions relating to Colonel Alon are relatively intact. Adam and Randy have been seeking the truth regarding the Alon murder for many years. Their assistance has been invaluable in putting pieces of the puzzle together. I cannot thank them enough for their help, and they deserve a lion's share of credit.

2. The West Coast also surfaced in the FBI files with the Black Panther allegations to the case.

3. State Department declassified files obtained under FOIA.

4. After the Munich Massacre, the State Department implemented Operation Boulder, a U.S. visa screening system to keep suspected Palestinian terrorists out of the country. The program ran from 1972 to 1975. On April 26, 1975, the *New York Times* ran a story on the program being shut down. Based on the past of Ali Hassan Salameh, and some would add that of PLO chairman Yasser Arafat, neither would have qualified for a U.S. visa due to

their terrorist ties. However, the State Department can authorize visas for foreign policy and intelligence considerations. On a practical level, it takes a U.S. government agency (State, CIA, FBI) to sponsor the visa applicant and explain why the visa should be issued. There are also exceptions granted for visits to the United Nations.

5. Ironically, Robert Ames was killed in the Hezbollah bombing of the U.S. Embassy in Beirut. Ames is believed to have been the CIA agent used by David Ignatius in his book *Agents of Innocence*, which may be the best novel I have read on terrorist informants.

6. The author spoke to David Ignatius and Robert Baer, former CIA agent, about Ali Hassan Salameh's relationship with the CIA. I also filed a Freedom of Information request with the CIA on Salameh, but the CIA response was "no record." Such a response agrees with the CIA's desire to protect their sources and was what I expected. The Israeli Aaron J. Klein in his book *Striking Back: The 1972 Munich Olympics Massacre and Israel's Deadly Response* (New York: Random House, 2005) and Dan Raviv and Yossi Melman in *Every Spy a Prince: The Complete History of Israel's Intelligence Community* (Boston: Houghton Mifflin, 1990) also discuss the CIA relationship with Salameh. These two books are wonderful and detailed reads on Mossad operations.

CHAPTER 17

1. Stan Orenstein and I have talked about this conversation on many occasions. Unfortunately, Stan cannot recall the name of the Mossad agent at the scene of the murder, and he took no notes about the conversation. The Mossad station chief in D.C. at the time of the killing was Ephraim Halevy. Stan also believes Halevy was at the crime scene. It is important for readers to understand that meeting off the record is not unusual in the least; rather it is how the intelligence community operates. Whispered comments, off-the-record briefings, leaked information, unofficial contacts and intelligence are exchanged all the time in this format. This is as true today as it was in 1973.

2. Both Ed and I attempted to find evidence of a documented killing and failed. I also asked our brilliant Stratfor analysts to search for similar data; they also came up with nothing. It is possible the information is true but was never made public. Cyprus is the crossroads for intelligence service operations for a range of foreign intelligence services, terrorist transit, and safe havens.

3. In *My Home, My Land: A Narrative of the Palestinian Struggle* by Abu Iyad and Eric Rouleau (New York: Times Books, 1981), Abu Iyad discusses the carnage caused by Israeli bombing of Palestinian refugee camps. I view his fixation on the IAF bombings as his primary motive for specifically tar-

geting Joseph Alon. In many ways, to Abu Iyad, Alon must have been a perfect military target.

4. Legal and operational security concerns mandate that I cannot disclose the killer's identity. Hassan Ali is an alias.

5. Our Beirut sources cannot be identified; doing so would put their lives at risk. Many of the sources are very close to the Ali family and cannot leave Lebanon. There is no doubt that Hezbollah would kill the informers if their identities were known.

6. FBI teletypes identify the Middle Eastern professor.

7. I did notify trusted contacts in the U.S. and Israeli intelligence services in an effort to hunt the suspect down. The reality is the case was simply too old and nobody had any historical knowledge. Cases like this are not career enhancing; nor do they get you promoted. In fact, the reverse is true; cases like this usually get you in trouble. The lack of help was not surprising. Some working agents view the Brazilian secret services as anti-Semitic, although no one will formally admit it.

8. I also knew that Imad Mugniyah had been assassinated in Damascus, Syria, in all probability by Mossad. Old scores had been settled, and Imad Mugniyah was crossed off my list.

9. The protection of diplomats today by the State Department Diplomatic Security Service and U.S. Secret Service is nothing like it was in 1973. In many ways, Alon was a soft target. After his murder, the Israeli diplomats in Bethesda, Maryland, moved into the high-rise apartments on the District line; one such apartment building is called The Irene. The Irene is located in the Friendship Heights area of Bethesda near the District of Columbia line.

10. Abu Iyad states in *My Home, My Land* that, in August 1973, there were two attempts on his life in Cairo, Egypt; one involved a young man with a silenced pistol and the other, a bomb in a briefcase. I think these were Mossad's ill-fated efforts to settle the score.

BIBLIOGRAPHY

Bar-Zohar, Michael, and Eitan Haber. *Massacre in Munich: The Manhunt for the Killers behind the 1972 Olympics Massacre.* Guilford, CT: Lyons Press, 2005.

Bregman, Ahron. *Israel's Wars: A History since 1947.* New York: Routledge, 2010.

Burton, Fred. *Ghost: Confessions of a Counterterrorism Agent.* New York: Random House, 2008.

Felt, Mark, and John O'Connor. *A G-Man's Life: The FBI, Being Deep Throat, and the Struggle for Honor in Washington.* New York: Perseus, 2006.

Goldman, Adam and Randy Herschaft. "Papers Shed Light on Envoy's '73 Killing." Associated Press, June 30, 2007.

———. "CIA, FBI Documents Provide Clues to 1973 Killing of Israeli Diplomat." Associated Press, June 30, 2007.

———. "AP IMPACT: Freedom Looms for Terrorist." Associated Press, January 25, 2009.

———. "Black September Terrorist Deported to Sudan." Associated Press, March 4, 2009.

Halevy, Efraim. *Man in the Shadows: Inside the Middle East Crisis with a Man Who Led the Mossad.* New York: St. Martin's Griffin, 2006.

Iyad, Abu, and Eric Rouleau. *My Home, My Land: A Narrative of the Palestinian Struggle.* New York: Times Books, 1981.

Jonas, George. *Vengeance: The True Story of an Israeli Counter-Terrorist Team.* New York: Simon & Schuster, 1984.

Klein, Aaron J. *Striking Back: The 1972 Munich Olympics Massacre and Israel's Deadly Response.* New York: Random House, 2005.

Mangold, Tom. *Cold Warrior: James Jesus Angleton: The CIA's Master Spy Hunter.* New York: Simon & Schuster, 1991.

Ostrovsky, Victor, and Claire Hoy. *By Way of Deception: The Making and Unmaking of a Mossad Officer.* New York: St. Martin's Press, 1990.

Raviv, Dan, and Yossi Melman. *Every Spy a Prince: The Complete History of Israel's Intelligence Community.* Boston: Houghton Mifflin, 1990.

Reeve, Simon. *One Day in September: The Full Story of the 1972 Munich Olympics Massacre and the Israeli Revenge Operation "Wrath of God."* New York: Arcade, 2000.

INDEX